PN   05870
1031   ADAMS
.A28   Contexts of poetry

Hazard Adams MICHIGAN STATE
UNIVERSITY

THE
CONTEXTS
OF
POETRY

Little, Brown and Company

BOSTON   TORONTO

FOR C.S.A. AND P.W.A.

SECOND PRINTING

Acknowledgments

THE AUTHOR is extremely grateful to the following publishers and agents for permission to quote from the works listed:

MRS. ROBERT S. ADAMS for the sonnet from "Animus Redundant" by Robert Simeon Adams.

BEACON PRESS for the quotation from *Symbolism and Belief* by Edwyn Bevan.

CHATTO & WINDUS LTD. for lines from "Legal Fiction" from *Collected Poems* by William Empson.

CONTACT PRESS for lines from "The Capture of Edwin Alonzo Boyd" by Peter Miller. Reprinted by permission of the author.

DODD, MEAD & COMPANY for lines from "To One in Bedlam" by Ernest Dowson from *The Poems of Ernest Dowson*.

FABER AND FABER LTD. for the quotations from *Collected Shorter Poems* and *Nones* by W. H. Auden; for quotations from *Collected Poems* and *Selected Essays* by T. S. Eliot; and for the selection from "The Love Song of J. Alfred Prufrock" by T. S. Eliot.

HARCOURT, BRACE & WORLD, INC. for selections from *Modern Man in Search of a Soul* by Carl G. Jung; for selections from "Tradition and the Individual Talent" and "The Metaphysical Poets" from *Selected Essays, 1917–1932* by T. S. Eliot; for lines from "The Love Song of J. Alfred Prufrock" and "Ash Wednesday" by T. S. Eliot; for lines from "Legal Fiction" from *Collected Poems* by William Empson; for "Impressions" by E. E. Cummings, copyright 1923, 1951 by E. E. Cummings, and reprinted from *Poems 1923–1954* by permission of Harcourt, Brace & World, Inc.

HEINEMANN EDUCATIONAL BOOKS LTD. for quotations from *English and Scottish Ballads* edited by Robert Graves.

HOGARTH PRESS LTD. for the quotation from *New Introductory Lectures* by Sigmund Freud.

HOLT, RINEHART AND WINSTON, INC. for the quotation from *A Glossary of Literary Terms* by M. H. Abrams.

HOUGHTON MIFFLIN COMPANY for the selection from "Ars Poetica" by Archibald MacLeish.

THE JOHNS HOPKINS PRESS for quotations from *Selected Prose, Poems, Essays and Letters* by Stéphane Mallarmé (translated by Bradford Cook); and for selections from *Apollo and the Nine* by Carol Maddison.

ALFRED A. KNOPF, INC. for "Bells for John Whiteside's Daughter" and "Captain Carpenter." Reprinted from *Selected Poems* by John Crowe Ransom. Copyright, 1924 by Alfred A. Knopf. Copyright, 1952 by John Crowe Ransom.

LOUISIANA STATE UNIVERSITY PRESS for the quotation from *Freudianism and the Literary Mind* by Frederick J. Hoffman.

THE MACMILLAN COMPANY for quotations from *English and Scottish Ballads* edited by Robert Graves; for lines from "Poetry" by Marianne Moore; for "Leda and the Swan," reprinted with permission of the publisher from *Collected Poems* by W. B. Yeats, Copyright 1928 by The Macmillan Company, Copyright 1956 by Bertha Georgie Yeats; for "The Wild Swans at Coole," reprinted with permission of the publisher from *Collected Poems*, Copyright 1919 by The Macmillan Company, Copyright 1946 by Bertha Georgie Yeats; for "The Cold Heaven" reprinted by permission of the publisher from *Collected Poems of W. B. Yeats* by W. B. Yeats, copyright 1912 by The Macmillan Company, copyright 1940 by Bertha Georgie Yeats; for lines from "Leda and the Swan" (Ad Variorum edition), "Nineteen Hundred and Nineteen," and first lines of "The Lover," "Byzantium," "I See Phantoms of Hatred . . . ," "Among School Children," "The Municipal Gallery Revisited," "All Souls' Night," "Three Songs to the One Burden," and "Sailing to Byzantium."

MACMILLAN CO. OF CANADA for "Leda and the Swan," "The Wild Swans at Coole," "The Cold Heaven," and the lines from "Leda and the Swan" (Ad Variorum edition), "Nineteen Hundred and Nineteen," "The Lover," "I See Phantoms of Hatred . . . ," "Among School Children," "The Municipal Gallery Revisited," "All Souls' Night," "Three Songs to the One Burden," and "Sailing to Byzantium."

MILLS MUSIC, INC. for the lyrics to "St. James Infirmary." Copyright 1929 by Gotham Music Service, Inc. Copyright renewed 1957. Used by permission of the copyright owner.

NEW DIRECTIONS for 20 lines from the "Eighth Pythian Ode" from *Some Odes of Pindar* translated by Richard Lattimore, copyright 1942 by New Directions; for "Fu I" from *Selected Poems* by Ezra Pound, Copyright 1926, © 1957 by Ezra Pound; and for the quotation from Ch. I of *Seven Types of Ambiguity* by William Empson, all rights reserved. Reprinted by permission of New Directions, publishers.

W. W. NORTON & COMPANY, INC. for the quotation from *Poetry: A Modern Guide to Its Understanding and Enjoyment* (1959) by Elizabeth Drew; and for the quotation from *New Introductory Lectures* (1933) by Sigmund Freud.

OXFORD UNIVERSITY PRESS, INC. for quotations from *The Ballad of Tradition* by Gordon Gerould.

PHAIDON PRESS LTD. PUBLISHERS for the quotation from *The Mirror of Art* by Charles Baudelaire (translated by Jonathan Mayne).

PRINCETON UNIVERSITY PRESS for quotations from *Anatomy of Criticism* by Northrop Frye.

RANDOM HOUSE, INC. for lines from "Victor was a little baby" and "In Memory of W. B. Yeats" by W. H. Auden, copyright 1940 by W. H. Auden, and reprinted from *The Collected Poetry of W. H. Auden*, by permission of Random House, Inc.; for lines from "Prime" by W. H. Auden, copyright 1951 by W. H. Auden, and reprinted from *Nones* by W. H. Auden, by permission of Random House, Inc.; for "Auto Wreck" by Karl Shapiro, copyright 1941 by Karl Shapiro, and reprinted from *Poems 1940–1953* by Karl Shapiro, by permission of Random House, Inc.; for lines from "Essay on Rime" by Karl Shapiro, copyright 1945 by Karl Shapiro, reprinted by permission of Random House, Inc.

ROUTLEDGE & KEGAN PAUL LTD. for quotations from *Modern Man in Search of a Soul* by Carl Jung.

CHARLES SCRIBNER'S SONS for lines from "Ode to the Confederate Dead" from *Poems* by Allen Tate. Used by permission of Charles Scribner's Sons.

SHAPIRO, BERNSTEIN & CO. INC. for the lyrics to "Ugly Chile" (originally "Pretty Doll") by Clarence Williams, copyright 1917 by Shapiro, Bernstein & Co. Inc. Copyright renewed and assigned. Copyright 1946 by Shapiro, Bernstein & Co. Inc., New York. Used by permission.

RUTH STAUFFER for lines from "The Lemmings" by Donald Stauffer.

ALAN SWALLOW for quotations from *Collected Essays* by Allen Tate. Reprinted by permission of the publisher, Alan Swallow. Copyright 1949, 1959 by Allen Tate.

UNIVERSITY OF CALIFORNIA PRESS for portions of C. F. MacIntyre's translations of *Correspondences* by C. Baudelaire and "Fantasy" by G. Nerval from *French Symbolist Poetry;* and "Ses Purs Ongles . . ." by S. Mallarmé from *Selected Poems of Mallarmé.*

UNIVERSITY OF CHICAGO PRESS for quotations from *Elizabethan and Metaphysical Imagery* (Phoenix edition) by Rosemond Tuve. Copyright 1959 by The University of Chicago.

UNIVERSITY OF NORTH CAROLINA PRESS for quotations from *Modern Poetry and the Tradition* by Cleanth Brooks.

A. P. WATT & SON for "Leda and the Swan" in full, together with some lines of the version found in the Ad Variorum edition; "The Wild Swans at Coole," and "The Cold Heaven" in full; portions of "Three Songs to the One Burden" and "Nineteen Hundred and Nineteen"; and the first lines only of "The Lover," "Byzantium," "I See Phantoms of Hatred . . . ," "Among School Children," "The Municipal Gallery Revisited," "All Souls' Night," and "Sailing to Byzantium." Reprinted from *Collected Poems of W. B. Yeats.*

YALE UNIVERSITY PRESS for quotations from *Essay on Man* by Ernst Cassirer.

MRS. W. B. YEATS for "Leda and the Swan," "The Wild Swans at Coole," "The Cold Heaven," and the lines from "Leda and the Swan" (Ad Variorum edition), "Nineteen Hundred and Nineteen," "The Lover," "Byzantium," "I See Phantoms of Hatred . . . ," "Among School Children," "The Municipal Gallery Revisited," "All Souls' Night," "Three Songs to the One Burden," and "Sailing to Byzantium."

Preface

THIS BOOK is meant primarily for college courses in the study of poetry. I have designed it for use along with a good anthology of English and American poetry and, perhaps, a glossary of literary terms.

Introductory courses in poetry have generally been of two sorts. The first and older is the survey of English literature, in which poetry is often lumped with other literary forms and emphasis is placed upon literature as a reflection of the age in which it was produced. The second sort is the course which emphasizes the reading and understanding of the poetic text through explication and the analysis of poetic devices with little or no attention paid to historical perspective. Neither of these approaches is adequate in itself, though of the two the second is, I think, more practical in the classroom. This book attempts to treat poetry formally, as in the second approach, but with attention to development. The emphasis, then, is upon the poem as a work of art meaningful only within a total view of poetry. This principle was clearly enunciated by T. S. Eliot in 1917:

> No poet, no artist of any art, has his complete meaning alone. His significance, his appreciation is the appreciation of his relation to the dead poets and artists. You cannot value him alone; you must set him, for contrast and comparison, among the dead. I mean this as a principle of aesthetic, not merely historical, criticism.[1]

[1] "Tradition and the Individual Talent," *Selected Essays, 1917–1932*, New York, 1932, pp. 4–5.

That last sentence should be carefully noted. The poem exists *in*
literature, as a part of it, and can be understood fully *as a work of
art* only in that context.

It is clear that a single book, and a small one at that, cannot do
more than approach understanding so conceived. It must devise
short cuts, allow itself to oversimplify, and simply pass over some
important matters. What it can do is keep alive throughout its
commentaries the sense of the poem as a work of art of a particular
kind produced at a particular stage of literary history — the sense
of the contexts in which the poem may profitably be viewed. As a
result of this emphasis the present book contains seven chapters
(2 through 8) devoted to kinds of poems, each chapter emphasizing a certain major period in the development of that kind of
poem. In Chapter 3, for example, the subject is the sonnet as a
verse form; the period emphasized is the late sixteenth and early
seventeenth centuries (although the sonnet's development from
Dante to Yeats is discussed); and the aspect of poetry under consideration is the poem as an artifice, rather than as, say, a form of
communication. Each chapter has a similar organization, with
most of the major periods of literary history treated. It is to be
noticed that the kinds of poems discussed are different in themselves. The sonnet is a verse form; the symbolist lyric is not limited
to a particular verse form but is characterized by its structure of
imagery; the metaphysical poem is conceived of on another level
as a poem of certain stylistic characteristics, though it could at the
same time be a sonnet with symbolist tendencies. The effort of
the seven chapters is to approach poetry in a variety of ways, at
the same time providing a sense of the continuity called for by
Eliot. The book has been greatly influenced not only by the principle he enunciated but also by the work of many modern critics
of sometimes contradictory persuasions. Some of these are M. H.
Abrams, Cleanth Brooks, Northrop Frye, I. A. Richards, and Donald Stauffer.

Ultimate emphasis in any course introducing poetry should be
on how to read a poem. It is likely that the teacher wishes to spend
his class time on specific poems and matters of poetic technique.

I should guess that particularly in respect to the latter he has found no amount of written description an adequate substitute for his own patient oral analysis of rhythm and other techniques. I therefore have felt that this book should pass beyond those elements of poetry that the teacher himself would rather explain directly and more effectively before the class. For the same reason I have not chosen, except in a few instances, to provide lengthy explications of poems; and in every case I have left plenty of room for further discussion. The one element which I stress throughout is "tone of voice," that quality of the poem most difficult to analyze, but upon which understanding of any poem ultimately depends. Where a poem is merely mentioned, the student, of course, should find the poem and read it in the light of the whole chapter.

It is evident, then, that this book does not provide a "course" in poetry but is meant as an accompaniment to the teacher's own presentation. In my own experience the material of Chapters 2 through 8 has been useful after a lengthy period devoted to introductory discussions of poetic technique and analyses of certain carefully chosen illustrative texts. *After that* I have found it useful to treat poetic form in terms of convention. The student may be helped through the earlier phases of study by the discussions of the few poems included in Chapter 1. I am hopeful that the chapter will also lay to rest certain common delusions about the nature of poetry. The last chapter, on the other hand, steps out and beyond the course in poetry to a consideration of the whole art of which poetry is a part. Its aim is to bring the considerations of poetry together in a general theory, adequate or inadequate as it may seem. If the teacher is to deal with the reading of poetry in his course he will probably not have time to take up such questions as the last chapter ponders, except as they arise here and there through the term's work. But that means only that he is doing his job well. The last chapter is meant then to lead the reader into considerations beyond the scope of the course in poetry itself, into the area where we question for ourselves the reasons for the study we have just concluded. My decision to include the last chapter is consistent with my aim throughout — to ask of the student an exertion

equal to that demanded of him by a text in philosophy or mathematics or one of the other humanistic disciplines. For the study
of poetry *is* a discipline and not for the faint-hearted.

HAZARD ADAMS

East Lansing, Michigan

Table of Contents

xiii

1 *Poems and Judgment:*

THE BEAUTIFUL AND THE AGREEABLE

Reading as a critical act. Coleridge's distinction between the beautiful and the agreeable. Richards' reading experiment. Cummings' poem as a "beautiful" structure. Allusion and ambiguity in a sonnet. Construing tonal meaning in Ransom's poem. Irresponsible use of language in Coffin's poem. The direction of this study.

1

One of the aims of a course in literature, and the principal aim of any study of the liberal arts, should be the development of a maturity of judgment, the ability to make decisions about things and to stand, at the same time, outside those decisions and observe them dispassionately — the ability, in other words, to make a critique of one's own criticisms. This is true in art as well as politics, in critical judgments about literature as well as decisions in moral philosophy, in economics, and in the polling booth. In literature courses we usually study the acknowledged great literary works; we less often study why they are great, a question that should not be evaded. Answering this question sometimes requires that we look at works of lesser merit and try to decide on what grounds we rank certain works above others. Why, really, do we value Robert Frost more than the verse in the "poetry corner" of our daily newspaper? Why do we value some of Frost's poems more highly than others? These are difficult questions. They involve some difficult probings of our own mental habits, some hard read-

1

ing and intellectual wrestling with the poems. Sometimes, when we examine our own interpretations and judgments of a poem we find out things about ourselves not necessarily pleasant. But that is the traditional end of a quest for knowledge. "Know thyself," the philosophers say, and the act of criticism is a means to carry one forth on that quest.

Literary study aims at these goals through the improvement of the reader's literary judgment. Such improvement comes about first through the reader's increased ability to construe verbal meaning, but also through his becoming acquainted with poetic conventions and the whole verbal universe which is poetry. It comes about, too, through his disabusing himself of certain preconceptions about what poetry should do; and that is the immediate subject here. One of the greatest English literary critics was the poet Samuel Taylor Coleridge (1772–1834). In his *On the Principles of Genial Criticism* (1814), he made a sensible distinction between the agreeable and the beautiful which has influenced critical thought ever since. A thing is agreeable for one or both of two reasons. The agreeable, he says, "involves a preestablished harmony, between the organs and their appointed objects." [1] The color green, for instance, may be agreeable to some people. Or, something may be agreeable by force of habit or by recalling to our minds a related pleasure. In our everyday speech we are inclined to use the word "beautiful" where we should, according to Coleridge, use the word "agreeable." Now it is fairly clear that a poem is not a good poem only because it is agreeable. The word for the most agreeable known color endlessly repeated would not constitute a poem, to say nothing of a *good* poem. Nor would something agreeable to one person through habit (such as a cigar) necessarily be agreeable to another. There must be some other criterion for judgment of the objective worth of the poem. Coleridge develops the criterion of the "beautiful": "That in which the *many*, still seen as many, becomes one." He proceeds to illustrate this somewhat cryptic assertion as follows:

[1] *Selected Poetry and Prose* (Elisabeth Schneider, ed.), New York, 1951, p. 373.

Take a familiar instance, one of a thousand. The frost on a win-
dow-pane has by accident crystallized into a striking resemblance
of a tree or a seaweed. With what pleasure we trace the parts, and
their relations to each other, and to the whole! Here is the stalk
or trunk, and here the branches or sprays — sometimes even the
buds or flowers. Nor will our pleasure be less, should the caprice
of the crystallization represent some object disagreeable to us.

The frost on the pane is Coleridge's metaphor here for a successful poem. Poetry "is an art . . . of representing, in words, external
nature and human thoughts and affections, both relatively to human affections, by the production of as much immediate pleasure
in parts, as is compatible with the largest sum of pleasure in the
whole." Coleridge is concerned, then, with the poem as a "beautiful" structure of words exhibiting a harmonious organization. His
consideration that the agreeable and disagreeable are both irrelevant to our sense of the beautiful must give us pause. We have
often shied away from works of art which have seemed on superficial acquaintance disagreeable to us. But a little reflection tells
us that disagreeable scenes take place in art of the very highest
order (in Sophocles' *King Oedipus* and Shakespeare's *King Lear*,
to say nothing of the carnage of the last scene of *Hamlet*). Death
is disagreeable, but it is the subject of much meditative verse. Injury and maiming, swearing and even obscenities occur in literary
works of the highest merit and are often necessary to the whole.
By the same token, agreeable things may not necessarily be beautiful. I, myself, find pictures of cuddly kittens on the covers of
women's magazines not beautiful or even particularly agreeable,
but the editors obviously put them there because most people
enjoy looking at them. I can appreciate the feelings of a lady I
overheard in the Louvre, who, looking at a picture of John the
Baptist's head on a platter (a favorite subject of painters at one
time in history), exclaimed: "I've been all over Europe, and I'm
sick and tired of heads being dished up on plates!" Nevertheless, I
for one prefer the heads on plates I have seen in the Louvre to the
sentimental kittens that stare at me from every supermarket maga-
zine counter.

Coleridge's distinction has been taken up by a twentieth-century literary critic, I. A. Richards, in his illuminating book *Practical Criticism* (1929). He describes there student reactions to several poems which he presented to them devoid of their titles, authors' names, and dates of composition. The students were without benefit of hints as to how they should react — "Oh, that's by Shakespeare; it must be good." They found themselves alone, confronting only the words on the page. Their judgments reveal considerable confusion in their critical standards. They were prone to "stock responses" based upon ingrained habit, to sentimentality (emotion in excess of the objects that the poem presents), to irrelevant associations caused by wholly personal experiences, to simple misconception of meaning. They revealed a general inability to make the very distinctions with which Coleridge was concerned. Furthermore, those who evoked standards beyond their sense of the agreeable did so upon some superficial idea of what a poem should be. If the poem was not composed in a recognized meter or clearly rimed, it was often thought not properly a poem. One notes that Coleridge's definition of "poetry" contains no technical rules that the poet must observe. Most critics who have set down such rules have lived to see a great poet violate their strictures.

II

With all this asserted but not done with, I should like to present at the outset an apparently unconventional poem by an American poet of established reputation. The purpose is to follow through with Coleridge's distinctions and his definition and show what can be known about the poem, how it can be read.

        stinging
        gold swarms
        upon the spires
        silver

            chants the litanies the
        great bells are ringing with rose

the lewd fat bells
             and a tall

wind
is dragging   10
the
sea

with

dream

–S   15

In respect to verse form the poem is unusual, but I shall try to
demonstrate that it is nevertheless very tightly constructed. Let
us take it stanza by stanza (there are six of them). We notice that
the first stanza is full of a buzzing alliteration which suggests, along
with the words "stinging" and "swarms," a mass of bees. The mention of gold, the color of bees, also adds to the suggestion. And yet
the stanza is not about bees. Bees are suggested to indicate, apparently, the quality of light as it strikes upon the spires of a
building. The light is conveyed to us not only visually but by a
synæsthesia — the mixture of sense impressions in a single image,
in this case the use of a buzzing swarm to describe primarily a sight
impression. The whole stanza is probably best taken as a single
sentence with "gold" the subject and "swarms" the verb. The "gold
swarms upon the spires" with the result that their silver color
stands out brightly. The gold is undoubtedly the sunlight which
reflects itself upon silver spires at a particular time of day. But the
poet chooses for us to pause slightly at the end of each line, and
we read each line alone as if it carried its own completed sensation. Thus the stanza's form allows for a tension between the unit
of sensation in each line (as if each line were an ejaculation) and
the complete sentence of the whole stanza.

A third complication arises with the second stanza, which begins
with a verb but in the middle of a line. This suggests that the subject can be "silver" ("silver chants the litanies"), or that the whole
of the first stanza, taken as a single situation, is chanting. A third,
and more likely, possibility is that the author wants no particular

subject but instead simply the impression of the *act* of chanting —
hence, a sentence without a subject. A similar impression is conveyed by line 1 of the first stanza ("stinging"), taken alone.

A litany is a liturgical prayer composed of invocations and sup-
plications with responses between clergy and congregation. This
chanting may well be meant to suggest the response of the silver
of the spires to the swarming buzz of sunlight — the convergence in
a single impression of light and spires. In any case, from the mention of chants and spires it is clear that a church is involved.

As if the poet wished to indicate the great rapidity of the impressions which the poem conveys, a second sentence seems to
begin after "litanies" before the close of the stanza's first line and
to proceed through the rest of the poem. The line can also be read,
however, with the word "which" implied after "litanies" so that
it is the bells which are sounding forth with the chant. Synæsthesia
is again the central device. The "bells are ringing with rose." The
modulation of color is evident throughout the poem — from gold
to silver to rose, thence to a colorless distant cold image of the sea
at night. The synæsthesia, of course, primarily suggests the nature
of the bells' sound. Silver will not do for that! The bells are resonant. But the color suggested also conveys a rapid changing of the
nature of the light at sunset. The whole impression is one of resonance in both sound and sight. Supporting this may be the suggestion of rose-shaped church windows reflecting light.

The change of light and the sound, however, is really, our poem
tells us, too much, too "colorful," too sticky sweet, almost obscene;
and the bells are described as lewd. (Is there here a suggestion of
fat, perhaps Chaucerian, monks, dressed in their usual robes so
that their shapes are those of bells?) In any case, the poet seems
to be concerned now with describing an extremely rich experience
of light and sound, which is so senuously full as to be excessive.
The image is comical and rightly so. But that impression also passes
quickly. With "and" a new sensation emerges. We are made to
dwell upon the opposite impressions conveyed by "tall," which
ends a line but belongs syntactically to the word "wind" in the
next stanza. Hanging on that spare, lean word and suddenly dis-

carding the fat bells and their almost sickening synæsthesia of rich sound and color, we enter very suddenly a world apparently of no color whatever. The wind dragging the sea occurs probably out of the range of the senses. It is also an interior image: that is, the mind of the perceiver seems to retire at this point into itself and call up a distant image, as if the thinker feels that he is suddenly detached from his senses and living only in himself. As the sentence proceeds it elongates, until finally each word becomes a separate stanza. And ultimately only one letter, the last letter of the last word alone as a stanza, finishes the poem. It is as if the thinker finds it difficult to complete his thought. The retirement into the mind is complete, however; the sunset is over. The perceiver is asleep, "sawing wood," for the last "–S" must be pronounced "Z," the traditional comic-strip way to signify snoring. That "Z" also completes the change of impression with which the poem is concerned by completing the modulation of the impression: the sibilant alliteration of the first stanza culminates in the softer "Z." We may notice also that even the shape of the poem on the page reflects its movement. It grows fat; its lines elongate in the resonant parts and shorten almost to nothing as the impression fades.

To many people, used to thinking that poetry always comes in quatrains or couplets of good old iambic pentameter, this poem will merely be disagreeable. And the unpleasantness will probably be accentuated by the intrusion of "lewd fat bells" upon the scene and the light-hearted use of "–S." But no judgment of this kind is fair or informed. The first important question is, "What is going on here?" When we ascertain roughly what this poem seems to be doing, then we can proceed to a judgment of its parts. Clearly the poem is much more carefully put together than many poems of conventional rime, rhythm, and diction. There is hardly an effect or an image or a placement of a word which, if I am right in the interpretation, has no function. And the poem's tone is carefully held to suggest the flux of impressions during a sunset, even to the flippantly comical description of the bells, which is *meant* to be excessive. The poem sustains this tone to the very end. The experience, though for a moment excessive, has been on the whole pleasant (a good poem *can* be agreeable), and the poet is not going to hang false solemnity on it. He feels that if it is anything, it is grounds for gaiety or at least whimsicality.

The author is E. E. Cummings (1894–1962), the title of the poem is "Impression." One senses that a single basic analogy gives the whole its shape. That is the analogy of French impressionistic painting, the paintings of Rouen Cathedral or the haystacks by Monet, for example. Even if the poem is eccentric, it has form. If the poem includes the disagreeable, which in another context we might properly reject, it is contained adequately within its form. The poem, in an extreme fashion, indicates also that poetry is beyond doubt an *art* of *words*; that the poet must bring words to heel; that he is a maker of objects composed of words, not simply the source of an unrestrained divine madness. In the act of "producing as much immediate pleasure in parts as is compatible with the largest sum of pleasure in the whole," the poet is rarely any better than his ability to construct with words will allow.

III

At the beginning of a course of study in literary theory recently, I made an experiment similar to that of I. A. Richards in *Practical Criticism*. My conclusions about readers corroborate his. I think it may be illuminating to examine three poems which I used in the experiment and summarize the conclusions. The first poem, a sonnet, evoked a great variety of commentary and almost as much perplexity.

> I am no Prince of Darkness, Lord of Sorrow,
> Perhaps Narcissus gazing in a pool,
> Or Hamlet fearing his own dead tomorrow
> In Yorick's skull — alas, alas, poor fool.
> I am in love so often with reflection;   5
> I look upon the mirrors that will show
> Only the mind, a fixed and bright projection
> Caught in the shadows that the mirrors know;

Yet I have seen that undeceiving picture
Of phosphorescent bone, with sockets bare,　　　　　10
Only the fiery bone, rid of its vesture
Of mouth and eyelids, cheeks, and flowing hair,
And where the heart might kindle laughter's spark
Only two holes that deepened into dark.

Several readers found this poem, as one said, "so far above the average reader's level of comprehension that it loses its beauty entirely, to say nothing of the meaning." Other responses ranged from extremely favorable to scornfully derogatory. One reader confessed himself "impressed" without understanding the poem. Another was convinced that the poet simply "rattles on about nothing." Among others, at least one reader made the *agreeable* his criterion: "I think it is effectively written, but I read poetry simply for the pleasurable feeling I derive from it. This doesn't make me feel very pleasant." One wonders whether the writer of this comment really reads poetry at all, for how much poetry supplies the kind of pleasure of which he seems to be speaking? Surely not very much. Better for that sort of thing to try a Swedish massage. Coleridge, it is true, claimed that a poem gives pleasure, but the pleasure he described is intellectual satisfaction achieved through the intellectual apprehension of the beautiful as distinguished from the agreeable or disagreeable. The poem, by its subject, is not likely to be agreeable, but we cannot simply reject all poems that discuss death, pain, and other disagreeable matters. Similarly it is ridiculous to accept poems about disagreeable subjects which evade the reality of experience by sentimental moralizing.

Nor will the rejection of the poem on grounds of difficulty quite do, either. Intellectual satisfaction is *achieved* satisfaction. Intellectual exercise, required of readers of poems, is no easier than any other sort of exercise. A poem certainly does not have to contain the verbal complexity of Cummings' "Impression" to be a good poem, but it must get at something significant in the human situation. Language is not a perfect tool, by any means. The poet's duty is to force language to reveal what is sometimes very nearly beyond its powers. Occasionally, perhaps very often, it will have to speak in a way not easy to follow. It may make demands upon the reader that he have read *Hamlet* (as this poem does) or some other work of literature. It may assume the knowledge of certain poetic conventions. The poet considers the language of all poetry his language, and he is not hesitant to employ allusion or conventions which have evolved their own suggestivity through repeated usage.

A great many charges of obscurity come not merely from ignorance but from intellectual sloth, sloppy reading, or insensitivity to nuance. This is not an easy poem, but that is only to say it may bear close reading and even some digging around. One can end up foisting off upon oneself a completely false meaning, based upon what a poem about the apprehension of death is expected to say. One of my students succeeded in doing just that: "The author is saying that although he has seen death and has had moments of unhappiness, he still likes to see the future as only bringing happiness. The aspect of death does not frighten him." Nothing could be further from the truth. I suspect that the reader has been led astray here not only because he wants to read a stock conclusion into the poem but also because he does not grasp the poem as a poem rather than as a moral assertion. Obviously few people want to fear death; therefore, the reader thinks the author will not "preach" the fear of death in his poem. One might remember at this point that the poet may be more interested in getting at the dramatic life of a situation than in drawing a moral from it. In this case the poem's speaker is offering no solutions but is instead meditating upon his own nature. The references to Hamlet and to Narcissus (who meditate, albeit in different ways, upon themselves) alone might lead one to believe this, but there are qualities of tone that make it certain. Some readers found it difficult to grasp the nature of the meditation and the tone simply because they lacked information. "Who is Yorick?" one of them asked, and another criticized particularly the fourth line as out of keeping with the tone of the whole.

Let us begin by supplying the necessary information. The Prince of Darkness, Lord of Sorrow, is, of course, the Devil. Narcissus is the figure from Greek mythology who fell in love with his own reflection in the water and gradually perished from the unapproach-ableness of the object of his love (see Ovid, *Metamorphoses* iii, for one version). The scene from *Hamlet* referred to in lines 3 and 4 is the famous graveyard scene (V, i). Hamlet, having returned to Denmark, comes upon the grave-diggers preparing Ophelia's grave. They have dug up the skull of old Yorick, court jester when Hamlet was a child. Hamlet picks up the skull and says, "Alas, poor Yorick! I knew him, Horatio; a fellow of infinite jest, of most excellent fancy," etc. This allusion is very important to the poem, for it explains the word "alas," which bothered many readers as too flamboyant and "poetic." In a rough paraphrase, the speaker declares that he is not the devil, not one who lives easily with dark-ness and sorrow, who dotes on it (if this were so the reader might well interpret his remarks as a fond dwelling upon man's mortality, a perverse love of dissolution). Instead he is perhaps Narcissus, in love with his own mortality, or Hamlet, possessed by thoughts of death as he gazes at Yorick's skull. Narcissus saw himself in the water. Hamlet saw his own "dead tomorrow" in Yorick's skull. He spoke of the jester, the court fool, with regret; but the speaker here makes that line ambiguous. The "poor fool" of the sonnet may be Yorick, but it may also be Hamlet; and finally it is the speaker himself — a fool for dwelling as he does upon death, a Lord of Sorrow after all. The speaker thus castigates himself for his own obsession. Part of the castigation is the accusation against himself that in the largest sense he is Narcissistic.

In philosophical and scientific discourse all ambiguities are scorned as obstructive to clear thought. But in literature, and par-ticularly in poetry, the possibility of double meanings, even multiple meanings, is always present. And often the poet operates by sug-gestion and implication. Such is the case here. And the poet is not yet done with the device, for he makes a pun on "reflection," a word picked up from the reference to Narcissus and developed in Hamlet's examination of Yorick's skull. Here it carries along that optical meaning, but it means primarily "contemplation"; for not only is the poet in love "perhaps" with his own mortality, but also he is enamored of thought upon it. The mirrors of the second quatrain pick up the reflection theme and apply it to the latter meaning of the word. He thinks upon the reality of himself and wants to discover it only in his mental or spiritual life. This part of the self is, however, as shadowy and elusive as Narcissus' image of his physical life was to Narcissus. That elusiveness makes reflection (contemplation) upon one's own mental life an endless quest and leads unfortunately to a kind of mental or spiritual Narcissism. The mind's image is clouded in the glass into which the speaker peers, and the longer he seeks for it the clearer becomes the "undeceiving picture" of his physical being, bright, persistent, and suggestive of his mortality. It forces its appearance to him in the form of his own skull, burning brightly in the mirror, and he is overcome by it. Reflection upon the mental life seems constantly to turn into reflection upon his own impending death. The mental life becomes as deceptive as Narcissus' image. Thought, then, has its own considerable terrors. At the climax the speaker's natural existence shines with such clarity and foreboding that for the moment at least it is the only reality. The sonnet suggests that the experience described is actually played out over and over again as the speaker vacillates between visions of the ideal mental life, which is always elusive, and the physical dying self, which brightly persists.

This sonnet, from the sequence *Animus Redundant* by Robert Simeon Adams (1897–1950), is, then, on a familiar theme. It employs allusion. In fact, its understanding depends upon its references to Hamlet and Narcissus and a grasp of the pun on "reflection."

IV

My next two examples are two dissimilar lyric poems. The first of these left almost half the readers completely puzzled, and very few of the others were able to grasp the poem fully:

> There was such speed in her little body,
> And such lightness in her footfall,
> It is no wonder her brown study
> Astonishes us all.

Her wars were bruited in our high window.   5
We looked among orchard trees and beyond
Where she took arms against her shadow,
Or harried unto the pond

The lazy geese, like a snow cloud
Dripping their snow on the green grass,   10
Tricking and stopping, sleepy and proud,
Who cried in goose, Alas,

For the tireless heart within the little
Lady with rod that made them rise
From their noon apple-dreams and scuttle   15
Goose fashion under the skies!

But now go the bells, and we are ready,
In one house we are sternly stopped
To say we are vexed at her brown study,
Lying so primly propped.   20

Unable to penetrate the poem's surface, readers frequently invented meanings. Several thought the poem was about a goose. One went so far as to think it about a goose lying on a dinner table at Thanksgiving. Once it was established that the poem concerned a dead little girl lying in her coffin before a funeral, readers found it extremely difficult to grasp the speaker's attitude toward her death. It is exactly there that the poem is most effective, I think. One reader reacted as follows: "I am unable to fully determine the proper meaning for the word 'vexed' (Are the people provoked, tormented, or worried?) and the interpretation of the final line 'Lying so primly propped.'" After reading several attacks on the poem for its obscurity and vagueness, I was pleased to find this reader striking, at least, to the center of the problem. The diction of this poem is its strength. The poet has sought for language that will convey very exactly the speaker's complex emotion at the death of a little girl whom he has often observed playing in the field beyond the orchard trees outside his window. The poet's attempt is to fix exactly the attitude of the speaker toward her death. He chooses as his scene the room in which her coffin lies, but we do not know this until we come to the last stanza, for the preceding

ones are cast into the form of remembrance which inhabits the
speaker's mind as he views her body. He is, of course, not really
speaking, but thinking. Indeed, his thoughts, cast into the edi-
torial "we," suggest those of all the adults viewing her body. The
remembrance stresses the distance between the observers and the
child, for the world of the child is remote from that of the adult.
In this case, the speaker has known the child best by observing her
from a distance through his window. And yet the distance does not
make the feelings of the speaker cold; it simply expresses his relationship to the deceased honestly and, in fact, enforces the total
sense of outrage at her death, for now the child is even more remote than she was when she inhabited the innocent world beyond
the orchard. The speaker simply cannot (or perhaps refuses to)
imagine her as she now is and calls her silence not death but a
"brown study," an expression denoting a kind of somber meditation wholly uncharacteristic of her. The surprising word "aston-
ishes" suggests at first not grief but pure surprise detached from
any other feelings. The poet wants to convey shock at the sudden
quietude of something that had seemed constantly to be in motion.
He keeps his poem on this abstract level — motion and stasis —
partly to avoid falling into the usual sentimental clichés about
dead children. In so doing, I think, he actually gives the grief a
greater dignity and universality than it might otherwise seem to
have.

In the child's world, wars are with shadows. Great heroic actions
are parodied. The third line of the second stanza recalls the line
from Hamlet's famous soliloquy (III, i), ". . . or to take arms
against a sea of troubles . . . ." There is something purposely ridiculous about wrenching it from that serious context and applying
it to the child — a sort of hyperbole, which points up her energy, her
complete absorption, her decisive manner — a parody of busy dedi-
cated adults. The poet makes the allusion with tender good nature.
She battles her shadow, harries not a sea of troubles but a flock
of honking, complaining geese. All of this is seen not in a picture
frame but a window, yet there is an analogy between the two which
the poet exploits to enforce the sense of distance, the geese formal-

ized (as in a painting) into a cloud, their droppings dotting the grass, moving in their arrogant way, complaining "in goose" — a language constructed out of the child's animated innocent world. Even though the child's world is remote, the contemplating adult views it tenderly and with an amused marveling respect suggested by the phrase "tireless heart."

With the last stanza, however, there is a sudden change, marked by the heavy movement of single syllable words and inversion of the normal word order. The bells toll in the line, and the speaker is now ready to go to the funeral; but in another sense he is ready only to admit vexation at the sight of the child "primly propped" in her coffin. Her primness is too unlike his window-framed "picture" of her, and the word "propped" suggests a doll-like unreality. The alliteration is slightly flippant and undercuts any suggestion of morbidity. Actually the image increases the shock. "Vexed" is a purposeful understatement which maintains the delicate sense of distance already established, suggests the universality of the situation, the indubitable, annoying fact of death. Not mawkishly grieving, the speaker chooses to be outraged, refuses to mention death. The poem is "Bells for John Whiteside's Daughter" by John Crowe Ransom (1888–   ). It is true, of course, that a title is part of a poem and no reader with the title before him would think the poem about a goose. Nevertheless, even without its title the poem should not mislead a careful reader.

In contrast to the development of a delicate tension between speaker and subject, between the various parts of the poem and between the feelings warring within the speaker, the next poem exhibits a considerable looseness and vagueness. Nevertheless, a good number of readers actually preferred it to the others:

> Love, the leaves are falling round thee;
>   All the forest trees are bare;
> Winter's snows will soon surround thee,
>   Soon will frost thy raven hair:
>   Then say with me,   5
>   Love, wilt thou flee,
> Nor wait to hear sad autumn's prayer;

          For winter rude
          Will soon intrude,
Nor aught of summer's blushing beauties spare.   10

Love, the rose lies withering by thee,
     And the lily blooms no more;
Nature's charms will quickly fly thee,
     Chilling rains around thee pour:
          Oh, then with me,   15
          Love, wilt thou flee,
Ere whirling tempests round thee roar,
          And winter dread
          Shall frost thy head,
And all thy raven ringlets silver o'er?   20

Love, the moon is shining for thee;
     All the lamps of heaven are bright;
Holy spirits glide before thee,
     Urging on thy tardy flight.
          Then say, with me,   25
          Love, wilt thou flee,
Nor wait the sun's returning light?
          Time's finger, rude,
          Will soon intrude
Relentless, all thy blushing beauties blight.   30

Love, the flowers no longer greet thee,
     All their lovely hues are fled;
No more the violet springs to meet thee,
     Lifting slow its modest head;
          Then say, with me,   35
          Love, wilt thou flee,
And leave this darkling desert dread,
          And seek a clime,
          Of joy sublime,
Where fadeless flowers a lasting fragrance shed? [2]   40

I suppose that most of the readers said they liked the poem because they could understand it (reduce it to a sensible paraphrase)
and because they recognized it as clearly what they thought a poem

[2] The reader will find this poem and a brief biography of the author in the
Cyclopædia of American Literature (E. A. and G. L. Duyckinck, ed.), Phila-
delphia, 1881, II, p. 33.

should be: flowery, about love, generous in its references to nature. Superficial familiarity in this case breeds an agreeable sense of security. The poem is, in addition, clearly rimed and moves with a rhythm obvious to the point of banality. Much bad poetry since the romantic period has all of these characteristics, and even today newspapers are likely to print such poems in their "poetry corners." Yet any discussion of this poem threatens to turn itself into a comic parody of it. Deep familiarity breeds contempt. Let us try a paraphrase: "Love, you are growing old. Therefore, come with me and enjoy love before it is too late." That is what the first stanza says. But what of the second stanza? It says the same thing, albeit a bit more urgently. The third stanza argues that angels are on the speaker's side, but the main point is the same. The fourth stanza makes the point again and promises a land of "joy sublime" where old age will not enter. Aside from the fact that the poet must repeat a point that needs only one expression, the means of statement is most unfortunate. Each stanza presents a figure for the coming of old age in terms of the seasons autumn and winter. The trouble with these figures is that they are too easy to take literally rather than only figuratively as the poet meant them. Therefore, in the first stanza the sensitive reader destroys the poem by calling up in his mind's eye the speaker's love standing in a barren forest with frost on her hair. In the second stanza this forest is populated with roses and lilies withered and dead, but now his love is being soaked by chilling rains. He repeats the threat of frost at the end of the stanza, and one has the vision of a veritable ice storm. One feels that the lady would surely have the sense to seek shelter before things came to this state of affairs.

Luckily, before issuing the threat of pneumonia the speaker shifts from his disastrous metaphor to one which, if safer, is even more innocuous and trite. It is now night. Holy spirits and the lamps of heaven are invoked. If his love cannot be convinced by the threat of torrents of rain and ice, can she be made cognizant of angels? During this whole metaphorical display the poet has been riming industriously, but sometimes at the expense of good sense and word order:

> Time's finger, rude,
> Will soon intrude
> Relentless, all thy blushing beauties blight.

Then we are returned to the flowers, but this time to a curiously acrobatic violet which "springs" to meet the speaker's love, at the same time "lifting slow its modest head," an unusual act which *The New Yorker* would call the neatest trick of the week. Now the speaker talks of his forest full of dead flowers and springing violets, snow and ice, as a desert. He recommends a "clime of joy sublime" (a rime on the moon-June level of tin-pan alley) and closes his poem. One can only conclude that the poet has nothing to say and says it at great length with no respect for economy or for the integrity of his poem as a whole. One has the impression that the poet has reached into a very small bag of poetic tricks and scattered the contents through four stanzas. I do not see how a judgment upon this poem (the author is Robert Coffin, 1797–1827) can be anything but derogatory, even if we judge it according to the agreeable rather than the beautiful — unless we assume that as a vehicle for daydreaming, a kind of mental Musak, it is to be read with absolutely no attention to the meaning of words. But poetry is an art of words, and words have meaning. The poet must make them work to the fullest of their powers and his own. I think it best, then, to begin the study of poetry with the assumption that the poet is a craftsman faced with a problem, the intransigence of words. It is not surprising that the traditional image for the poet is the Greek god Hephæstos, the blacksmith, maker of the armor of Achilles. His tool is the hammer, and he works by beating his material into shape. If we begin, then, with the assumption that the poem is an object that has been shaped according to Coleridge's principle of the beautiful, we shall be on the right road.

V

The next seven chapters take various approaches to kinds of poems, each emphasizing a particular historical period. The various approaches treat the poem, respectively, as public speech, as artifice, as argument, as imitation, as expression of character, as drama, and as a self-contained world. Throughout these chapters the effort is particularly to keep the eye upon the poem as a formal construction (according to Coleridge's definition and Eliot's stricture), which projects tone and attitude through the exact and intense use of words.

Some Suggested Reading

Coleridge, S. T., *Selected Poetry and Prose* (E. Schneider, editor), pp. 372–395.

Richards, I. A., *Practical Criticism*.

2 Ballad and Song:

POEM AS PUBLIC UTTERANCE

Emergence of popular ballads in the eighteenth century. Percy's Reliques. "Sir Patrick Spens" as an example. Rhythm, refrain, speaker's detachment. Popular songs. Nineteenth-century adaptations: Wordsworth, Keats, and others. Modern ironic usage: Auden and others. Jazz lyrics.

1

The kind of poetry most often studied in literature courses is not public in the same way as popular songs or folk ballads are; yet our poetry would not be what it is without the existence of a popular tradition. The poet is likely to assert, as does for example Robert Graves, that he writes only to the muse, to some ideal of artistic perfection; and this is no doubt true. He is an artificer, as I shall emphasize in Chapter 3, working with forms and conventions. But William Wordsworth (1770–1850) was certainly not totally wrong when he remarked that the poet is a "man speaking to men." [1] He was, indeed, at least half right, for the poet does write to people as well as create an object. He desires that his object be seen and appreciated. The revival of interest in popular ballads among poets has something to do with this interest and usually goes hand in hand with a drive toward simplicity of state-

[1] "Preface to Lyrical Ballads" (1800), *The Prelude, with a Selection from the Shorter Poems*, etc. (Carlos Baker, ed.), New York, 1954, p. 13.

ment and a pruning away of all poetic excess in general. Poets have been tantalized by the idea that ballads are, as Sir Herbert Read has written, the most fundamental and authentic type of all poetry. Indeed the ballad is one of the oldest forms of English poetry. Some examples survive from as early as the twelfth century. It is worth our while, therefore, to examine the relationship between poetry and the popular ballad at the outset of our study.

One cannot trust the history of the word "ballad" to explain what a ballad is. The poems we call ballads apparently came to be so named in the sixteenth century. We know that Hotspur in Part 1 of *Henry IV* refers to such ballads with a sneer, but as late as the fifteenth century the word seems not to have been used to describe ballads as we know them. "Ballad" comes from the Latin *ballare* — to dance. There were poems written in Italy called *ballata* (Rossetti translated some of Cavalcanti's). In France a poem called a *ballette* was a lyric of three stanzas and a refrain, related to the *chanson de carole*. And the "ballade" was a form used by Chaucer, who added to the *ballette* a fourth stanza or "envoy." But these poems have nothing to do with ballads as we know them. They are instead songs in various metrical forms, usually, as the derivation implies, associated with dances. The "ballade," or the kind of poem Chaucer wrote in "Hyde, Absolon, Thy Gilte Tresses Clere," has probably an older history than the ballad as we know it. In any case, by the eighteenth century (in the prose of Addison, for example) the meaning of "ballad" was fixed as a story told in song.

Until that time the ballad had existed independent of the main stream of poetry. The manner of transmission had been pretty generally oral. The ballad was looked upon with contempt by poets and critics, although Sir Philip Sidney in his *Apologie for Poetry* (1595) admitted the power of some of those with which he was familiar: "Certainly I must confesse my own barbarousnes, I never heard the olde song of *Percy* and *Duglas*, that I found not my heart mooved more than with a trumpet." Even in the eighteenth century when Bishop Percy made his famous collection of ballads, *Reliques of Ancient English Poetry*, he could not refrain from apologies for his undertaking:

This manuscript was shown to several learned and ingenious friends, who thought the contents too curious to be consigned to oblivion, and importuned the possessor to select some of them, and give them to the press. As most of them are of great simplicity, and seem to have been merely written for the people, he was long in doubt, whether, in the present state of improved literature, they could be deemed worthy of the attention of the public.

He proceeds to point out their strengths and weaknesses:

In a polished age, like the present, I am sensible that many of these reliques of antiquity will require great allowances to be made for them. Yet have they, for the most part, a pleasing simplicity, and many artless graces, which in the opinion of no mean critics have been thought to compensate for the want of higher beauties, and if they do not dazzle the imagination, are frequently found to interest the heart.

It is not surprising, if Percy's statement is correct, that in the eighteenth century the ballad should emerge as popular among the literati. A glance at Wordsworth's Preface to the second edition of the *Lyrical Ballads* (1800) shows us at once that "artless graces" which touch the heart are by that time the avowed aim of Wordsworth, ahead of his time but prophetic of the taste he helped to create.

II

Before proceeding to the kind of poetry that the ballad-influence helped bring into being, it is important to describe the ballad — the "popular ballad," or "ballad of tradition," as it has been variously called. Strict definition probably requires that a song or poem be called a ballad only when it is in oral circulation. Since most medieval ballads have now been written down and given a sort of final form in the editions of many ballad scholars, we would be left only with current ballads of fairly recent origin. Obviously we cannot so restrict ourselves. Let us instead accept as a beginning Gordon Gerould's definition in his *The Ballad of Tradition:* "A ballad is a folk song that tells a story with stress on the crucial situation, tells it by letting the action unfold itself in event and speech, and tells it objectively with little comment or intrusion of personal bias." [2] And now an example is necessary. But at once we are in difficulties, for ballads have several versions. Should we take the scholarly approach, as did F. J. Child in his famous collection, and offer several known versions of the same ballad, or should we choose the best version? Or should we do as Robert Graves has done in his collections and make a composite version?

> Most ballad anthologies published nowadays are "scholarly," which means that the editors feel obliged to print each ballad exactly as it occurs in one of the many variant versions still surviving. But unless such a version happens to be superior to all others in every stanza, this seems unjust to the reader, who is entitled to see the best text. Usually, therefore, I have combined several versions, choosing the most telling stanzas or phrases from each. [3]

Graves' argument may have something to recommend it, particularly when the editor is a poet of Graves' rank. In practice, however, at least in respect to the ballad I have chosen as an illustration, "Sir Patrick Spens," it is not effective. Graves' version is nearly twice as long as version "A" in Child's collection, adds a considerable amount of detail, enlarges on the story, and in so doing contributes to a general softening of the ballad's best features, which are its terse brevity of characterization and its ability to strike directly at the essential situation. In choosing all the "best" lines and stanzas, Graves has cluttered the poem and even in some cases made the story unlikely. Child's "A" text seems, after all, superior: [4]

> The king sits in Dumferling toune,
>   Drinking the blude-reid wine:
> "O whar will I get guid sailor,
>   To sail this schip of mine?"

[2] *The Ballad of Tradition*, Oxford, 1932, p. 11.
[3] *English and Scottish Ballads*, London, 1957, p. xxiv.
[4] Ballads are not the only poems which present textual problems. Many poems have more than one printed version, as in the case of Wyatt's sonnet, quoted in Chapter 3. Unless a clearly final manuscript exists, an editor must *make* a text rather than simply transcribe it.

Up and spak an eldern knicht,   5
   Sat at the king's richt kne:
"Sir Patrick Spence is the best sailor
   That sails upon the se."

The king has written a braid letter,
   And signed it wi his hand,   10
And sent it to Sir Patrick Spence,
   Was walking on the sand.

The first line that Sir Patrick red,
   A loud lauch lauched he;
The next line that Sir Patrick red,   15
   The teir blinded his ee.

"O wha is this has don this deid,
   This ill deid don to me,
To send me out this time o' the yeir,
   To sail upon the se!   20

"Mak hast, mak haste, my mirry men all,
   Our guid schip sails the morne:"
"O say ne sae, my master deir,
   For I feir a deadlie storme.

"Late late yestreen I saw the new moone,   25
   Wi the auld moone in hir arme,
And I feir, I feir, my deir master,
   That we will cum to harme."

O our Scots nobles were richt laith
   To weet their cork-heild schoone;   30
But lang owre a' the play wer playd,
   Thair hats they swam aboone.

O lang, lang may their ladies sit,
   Wi their fans into their hand,
Or eir they se Sir Patrick Spence   35
   Cum sailing to the land.

O lang, lang may the ladies stand,
   Wi thair gold kems in their hair,
Waiting for thair ain deir lords,
   For they'll se thame no mair.   40

Half owre, haf owre to Aberdour,
   It's fiftie fadom deip,

> And thair lies guid Sir Patrick Spence,
> Wi the Scots lords at his feit.[5]

In Child's version above, the reasons for Sir Patrick's being sent to sea in the treacherous season are not established. In Graves' version he is sent to bring the king's daughter back from Norway. This information raises the question of why the king should have entrusted his daughter to the dangerous seas and gives to Sir Patrick a specific destination. In "A" all this is left to our conjecture: Sir Patrick is merely ordered to sail his ship, and the emphasis is forcibly upon the necessity of his act according to the laws of fealty and his own dignity. "A," then, has the spareness which is a characteristic virtue of the good ballad. Graves, on the other hand, in an effort to include all the good lines, has sacrificed the effect of the whole. No known version (except Graves' own) attempts to include all the ramifications of the story. Each instead molds its own tale. In one, Sir Patrick asserts that he is not a good sailor, curses whoever suggested his name to the king:

> "O wha is this, or what is that,
>   Has tald the king a me?
> For I was never a good seaman
>   Nor ever intend to be."

In another, the crew arrives in Norway and carouses. They are not at all eager to return.

"Sir Patrick Spens" is a typical ballad. It is clearly a folk song that tells a story. Its many versions indicate a history of oral transmission. Its actions center on a single episode without any effort to fill in details of before and after. Rather than recounting the whole story, the narrator chooses only to emphasize particular moments in the action. Characters are not established through the building-up of detail but are presented by means of a few words, usually fixing our sense of the character in some momentary act. The narrator does not intrude upon his story, but maintains a discreet distance. Nor does he attempt any subtle poeticisms. His language

---

[5] *braid*: bold, straightforward, long; *laith*: loath; *cork-heild*: cork-heeled.

is generally commonplace and even filled with stock figures, phrases, and symbols, some of which appear frequently in other ballads. Wine, for example, is always "blood-red," horses are "steeds" — usually "milk-white." These commonplaces of phrase attest to the oral nature of the art and to the fact that there was quite naturally no tradition of criticism of the ballad, which might hold it back from dull diction and form.

It is clear that the ballad, though narrative in structure, is not epic in proportion, but is as the short story is to the novel. One sign of the poem's success is that it fixes in our imagination particular significant moments or makes incisive comments on a situation. In the first stanza of "Sir Patrick Spens" the king is presented in a cliché of balladry, but the juxtaposition of the king drinking the blood-red wine and at the same time deciding to send a good sailor on a hopelessly dangerous mission lends great force to the situation and establishes the nature of kingly power. The author does not explain the meaning of the coexistence of these two actions any more than does Ezra Pound in his short poem modeled on a Chinese poetic form:

Fu I loved the high cloud and the hill.
Alas, he died of alcohol.

in which the contrast of the two simple facts is allowed to sink into our consciousness.

A king's order might not have to be obeyed unless the person ordered were a coward or an unthinking vassal, or unless he thought that morally it should be obeyed. The fourth stanza begins to reveal briefly but incisively just what kind of man Sir Patrick is. We have already seen him receive the letter as he walks on the sand at his ease. The line places him near to the sea, suggests his love for it, perhaps evokes our sympathy with him. We are inclined to picture him as a thoughtful, meditative person. But he is also heroic. He first laughs, but the laugh changes to tears. Though the lines describing this are a ballad cliché, here they effectively express the two aspects of Sir Patrick's being which enable him to be a great sailor and a man honored by the court. He can see the situation both from within and without at the same time. He can laugh at the irony of the situation in which his own reputation as a brave and admirable sailor has forced a cruel choice upon him. He can obey the king as a true courtier and probably perish, or he can refuse and reject the very characteristic that led to his being chosen in the first place. Our first vision of Sir Patrick walking on the shore enforces our sense of his being alone with his decision. After the bitter perception of his fate (meanwhile the author gets in the information that it is winter), Sir Patrick bewails it; but not for long. When he is in the presence of his sailors none of his bitter feelings are evident to them, though we the readers know they must be there. He has made his decision to carry out the king's orders, and the poem shows him acting immediately. It does not fill itself out with details irrelevant to the central situation.

In contrast to Sir Patrick's complaint against his bad luck, the reaction of the sailors is generalized in lines of superstition and fear. At this point Sir Patrick's nature has been established. The denouement is certain, and the ballad proceeds to describe it with complete objectivity. The death of such a man does not demand a wailing poet. It contains its own tragedy without need of embellishment. The tragic is even played down in the direction of the bitterly comic:

> But lang owre a' the play wer playd,
> Thair hats they swam aboone.

Irredeemable *fact* is emphasized in the last stanza, where the narrator measures the exact amount of water above the Scots lords' heads — "fiftie fadom deep," the consonants thudding out the finality of their drowning.

Not many ballads in the Child collection have the unity and sophistication of this version of "Sir Patrick Spens." Nor is every ballad identical in metrical pattern and other matters of technique. The pattern of "Sir Patrick Spens" is a quatrain with alternating lines of four and three stresses. Gerould has pointed out that in many ballads of this kind the quatrain is best read as a rimed cou-

plet in which each line has seven stresses. He also has observed that
the stresses fall with heavy and lighter weight in strict alternation:

> $\overset{+}{\text{The}}$ $\overset{+}{\text{king}}$ $\overset{-}{\text{sits}}$ $\overset{+}{\text{in}}$ $\overset{}{\text{Dumferling}}$ $\overset{-}{\text{toune}}$,
>
> $\overset{+}{\text{Drinking}}$ the $\overset{-}{\text{blude-reid}}$ $\overset{+}{\text{wine}}$.

Albert Friedman has observed that this is because ballad tunes are
composed in compound time. As a consequence each bar has a
medial beat as well as a main beat at the beginning. The ballad's
rhythmic structure, we are constantly reminded, is the result of its
having been sung.

Another aspect of the ballad is the frequency with which it includes a refrain. The refrain of the following ballad does not, however, occur in all the collected versions:

> As I was walking all alone,
> *Down a down a down hey down*
> I heard twa corbies making a moan:
> The one unto the other say,
> "Where shall we gang and dine today?"
> *With a down, derry, derry, derry, down.*

> ("The Twa Corbies")

Unlike the refrains in carols, which support the poetic theme, ballad refrains are often sheer nonsense (as above) or incantatory.
Sometimes the ballad employs repetition of the last line of a stanza
or some sort of parallelism of phrase:

> "O where ha you been, Lord Randal, my son?
> And where ha you been, my handsome young man?"
> "I ha been at the greenwood; mother, mak my bed soon,
> For I'm wearied wi hunting, and fain wad lie down."

> "An wha met ye there, Lord Randal, my son?
> An wha met you there, my handsome young man?"
> "O I met wi my true-love; mother, mak my bed soon,
> For I'm wearied wi hunting, and fain wad lie down."

> ("Lord Randal")

And so on, through eight more stanzas of question and answer.
Lord Randal reveals that his "true love" poisoned him with "eels
fried in a pan." When the mother questions her dying son about
his will the refrain changes to:

> For I'm sick at the heart, and I fain wad lie down.

This ballad, like most, has a very rigid structure. As in much music,
repetition of the pattern builds up expectation, which makes even
a slight variation seem immensely significant. In the course of reading we learn that the son will leave his twenty-four cattle to his
mother, his gold and silver to his sister, and his houses and lands
to his brother. In the last stanza the balladeer does not have to intrude any remarks of his own to convey the bitterness of the young
lord:

> "What d'ye leave to your true-love, Lord Randal, my son?
> What d'ye leave to your true love, my handsome young
>   man?"
> "I leave her hell and fire; mother, mak my bed soon,
> For I'm sick at the heart, and I fain wad lie down."

The brevity of the curse and the repetition of the pattern give
force to the poem's conclusion. It is clear that this kind of repetition serves the artistic purpose of intensity. When the refrain is
nonsensical it is more difficult to explain except in the strictly
musical context of performance, where the nonsense may have
musical "meaning." Popular ballads, as the old lady said to Sir
Walter Scott, who was collecting them and writing them down,
were "made for singing and no for reading, but ye hae broken the
charm now and they'll never be sung mair." [6]

III

Scott, at the beginning of the nineteenth century, was not the first
to collect popular ballads. Three centuries before, a kind of balladeer's tin-pan alley developed in London and other cities. Hack

[6] Quoted by Albert Friedman in *The Viking Book of Folk Ballads*, New York,
1956.

rimers composed ballads and sold them on sheets of paper called broadsides. This practice tended to die out in England in the nineteenth century, but it was very popular in mid-nineteenth-century America. Broadside ballads were the popular ballads of urban society. Even today we often call our popular songs "ballads," though the term goes back to the old French *ballade*. Our popular songs usually have little relation to the popular ballad, even though they are a kind of counterpart to the old broadsides.

Sometimes, however, our popular songs do tell a story, as in a song made famous in the early 1940's by the King Cole Trio, telling about an eagle taking a monkey for a ride in the air and trying to throw him off his back, at which point the monkey admonishes the eagle to "straighten up and fly right." We never do discover what happens and are left in a "Perils of Pauline" situation. The refrain, repeated over and over, contains the admonishment, so that it performs more than a purely musical function. In most songs of this sort, as in most jazz, the music is more important than the words, and the singer is more or less another instrument.

Tin-pan alley may provide our urban "ballads" in America, but in rural districts genuine popular ballads have flourished. There are many cowboy and lumberjack ballads, ballads of the oil fields and the sea, of robbers, and, of course, those ballads of Negro origin allied closely to jazz. Many of these have a curious history. In his *Viking Book of Folk Ballads*, Albert Friedman traces the cowboy song "Streets of Laredo" and the Negro tune "St. James Hospital" ("Bad Girl's Lament") back to a ballad sung in Ireland about 1790 called "The Unfortunate Rake." [7] In that ballad the rake is dying of syphilis and orders a military funeral amid regrets and lamentations over his fate. Both the cowboy and Negro versions, reproduced by Friedman, are well known. They are in turn related to the jazz tune "St. James Infirmary Blues." In the Jack Teagarden-Louis Armstrong version the words go like this:

> O, I went down to St. James Infirmary,
> Saw my baby there, baby there,

[7] *The Viking Book of Folk Ballads*, pp. 424–425.

Stretched out on a long white table
So cold, so still, so fair,
Let her go, let her go, God bless her, 5
Wherever she may be.
She can look this whole wide world all over.
She'll never find another man like me.
Now when I die I want you to dress me in straight black
   shoes,
A box back coat and a Stetson hat, 10
Put a twenty-dollar gold piece on my watch chain
So the boys will know I died standin' pat.

The jazz lyric (to which I shall return), swing, and popular music
of all kinds are today's American broadsides. The poetic and musical qualities of these pieces probably vary even more than those
of the ballads collected by Child. And perhaps more than ever before these songs depend for their effect upon rendition.

IV

The ballad is not, as we have observed and defined it, an "art"
form. It has no tradition of criticism, and it was collected apolo-
getically by Percy. Nevertheless, from at least the late eighteenth
century it has had a very definite influence on the course of poetry.
It is not surprising that a period of neoclassicism, the so-called
"age of reason" of the eighteenth century, should evolve its
own opposite, a reaction against sophistication and artifice among
poets: "The principal object, then, proposed in these poems was
to choose incidents and situations from common life, and to relate
or describe them, throughout, as far as was possible in a selection
of language really used by men," wrote Wordsworth in the 1800
Preface to the second edition of his *Lyrical Ballads*. He was attacking the poetic diction, the "gaudiness and inane phraseology" of
a dying elegant mode of poetry. He saw in the ballad a form which
suggested the real language of men, a language in touch with
"humble and rustic life" ("in that condition the essential passions
of the heart find a better soil in which they can attain their maturity"), a poetic form which had in its very survival the sanction

of the people. The ballad, for Wordsworth, spoke "a plainer, more emphatic language" than the poetry of artifice and decoration.

Wordsworth appropriated the ballad form in three of its aspects. First, his poems are often balladic in verse form. His Lucy poems, for example, employ the popular ballad quatrain with alternating verses of four and three stresses. Second, he adopted the balladic simplicity of language as consistent with his principle of using "real" language. Third, he found the balladic tendency to tell a story only in its necessary lineaments, without flourish or explanation, useful to accomplishing his own purpose: to make the feeling give importance to the action rather than vice versa. But Wordsworth did something very rare in popular ballads. His speaker intrudes himself openly into the poem, not merely as a narrator but as the main actor in the drama. An example is "The Fountain," the first four stanzas of which follow:

> We talked with open heart, and tongue
> Affectionate and true,
> A pair of friends, though I was young,
> And Matthew seventy-two.
>
> We lay beneath a spreading oak,   5
> Beside a mossy seat;
> And from the turf a fountain broke,
> And gurgled at our feet.
>
> "Now, Matthew!" said I, "let us match
> This water's pleasant tune   10
> With some old border-song, or catch
> That suits a summer's noon;
>
> "Or of the church-clock and the chimes
> Sing here beneath the shade
> That half-mad thing of witty rhymes   15
> Which you last April made!"

Two other things unusual in the popular ballad are evident here. Wordsworth undoubtedly admired the simplicity of diction in the old ballads, but his own brand of dictional simplicity is certainly different. There is no recourse to clichés of balladry in order to establish ballad flavor. To do this would have been to fall into another kind of artificiality. Instead, Wordsworth endeavors to keep his eye on the object. He establishes the scene economically by showing us one or two things — the oak tree, the fountain, but nothing more. Indeed one of these objects has a symbolic purpose. He moves directly toward the central situation, which expresses Matthew's grief at his isolation, at his loss of his loved ones, at the knowledge of the difference between man and nature. The speaker of the poem, touched by Matthew's melancholy and moved to express his affection, makes an offer:

> "And Matthew, for thy children dead
> I'll be a son to thee!"
> At this he grasped my hand, and said,
> "Alas! that cannot be."

> We rose up from the fountain-side; 65
> And down the smooth descent
> Of the green sheep-track did we glide;
> And through the wood we went;

> And ere we came to Leonard's rock,
> He sang those witty rhymes 70
> About the crazy old church-clock,
> And the bewildered chimes.

The second difference from the popular ballad is the conscious use of symbols. Upon first observation the reason for calling the poem "The Fountain" is not clear. On the surface, the fountain appears to be introduced only to fill out the scene. The speaker mentions it to us, and also to Matthew, suggesting that they match the water's tune with their own. At first Matthew does not sing, but deplores his own (and Man's) separation from nature. After the speaker's offer and Matthew's rejection of it, he nevertheless does sing his gay, irrational song. He establishes himself as not quite so separated from nature as his earlier moping suggested. The fountain with its spontaneous overflow of water and sound is representative of the life of nature. When Matthew finally matches its song with his own "spontaneous overflow of powerful feelings," as

Wordsworth defined poetry in his Preface, he overcomes his own feeling of aloofness from the rhythm of nature. This he does, not through acceptance of the speaker's offer to become his son, but through acceptance of things as they are and must be. The poem is constructed about the symbolic object mentioned in the title, with a self-consciousness unknown to most popular ballads but with much of their simplicity.

Another aspect of Wordsworth's balladic poems bears mention. Consistent with his conception of the action giving importance to the feeling is the tendency of his poems to reach an "epiphanic" climax, in which both the speaker and reader experience a sudden illumination. This experience is seldom explained, but is instead communicated through the action itself and left in its immediacy for the reader to contemplate. The term "epiphany" is theological, meaning sudden manifestation of the supernatural. It was applied secularly to literature by James Joyce in order to describe the moment in a work of fiction where a situation comes clear and the reader, as it were, sees into the heart of a mystery. In "The Fountain" the image of Matthew singing his songs with tragic gaiety shifts our attitude toward him abruptly, but with an abruptness totally in keeping with the dramatic presentation. It is not that Matthew has changed; our understanding has been intensified in an unexpected direction. Our admiration for him exceeds the expected bounds *because* of the tragic background before which he sings his witty songs.

Quite often in Wordsworth the epiphanic moment turns upon an optical illusion of some kind, as in the boat-stealing and skating scenes from *The Prelude* (Book I). But these are not ballads. A balladic example occurs in one of the Lucy poems; the whole poem follows:

> Strange fits of passion have I known:
> And I will dare to tell,
> But in the Lover's ear alone,
> What once to me befell.
>
> When she I loved looked every day
> Fresh as a rose in June,

5

I to her cottage bent my way,
Beneath an evening-moon.

Upon the moon I fixed my eye,
All over the wide lea;   10
With quickening pace my horse drew nigh
Those paths so dear to me.

And now we reached the orchard-plot;
And, as we climbed the hill,
The sinking moon to Lucy's cot   15
Came near, and nearer still.

In one of those sweet dreams I slept,
Kind Nature's gentlest boon!
And all the while my eyes I kept
On the descending moon.   20

My horse moved on; hoof after hoof
He raised, and never stopped:
When down behind the cottage roof,
At once, the bright moon dropped.

What fond and wayward thoughts will slide   25
Into a Lover's head!
"O mercy!" to myself I cried,
"If Lucy should be dead!"

The speaker is careful to disclaim any rationality for his action. As a lover he acted as he would not have in some other mental state. The whole drama of the poem centers upon his astonishment at his own thoughts. He is, in fact, so astonished that he admits his unwillingness to tell his story except to another lover, who might be presumed to understand his state and not consider it absurd. The feelings, he is certain, are not unusual ones, but they are also not rational. An optical illusion is the outer source of the feelings. As the speaker moves along, his mind upon Lucy, his eye upon the moon, the two objects merge symbolically in his mind. In fact, he falls into a reverie in which he is detached from all but symbolic meaning. As he nears the cottage, the object of his stare drops out of sight. In a weird transference the thought that Lucy also is gone flashes through his mind. Even at this point he recognizes the illusory nature of the feelings. He is even perhaps embarrassed by them. The thought is "fond and wayward" and "slides" surreptitiously into the lover's mind. Even though the speaker rejects the thought as fanciful, the dramatic presentation, the slow building-up of the movement of the horse through the uniform balladic rhythm brings the reader into the *reality* of the speaker's illusion. There is, then, a double focus, that of the reason, with its reservations, and that of the passions. The poem's force lies in the tension between the two. Wordsworth makes use of simple unobtrusive imagery ("sweet as a rose in June") which does not call attention to itself and thus overcome the metronomic development of the speaker's self-hypnotic concentration on the moon.

V

Wordsworth's attachment to the balladic form arose from his attempt to revolutionize poetic diction and return to the language of the people. Other poets of his time also found the ballad to their liking, sometimes for other reasons. The reaction against neoclassicism resulted in a glorification of the medieval. We see it in Keats' "Eve of St. Agnes," but it is in his famous "La Belle Dame Sans Merci" that the medieval trappings are combined with balladic stanzas. Keats' conception of language is not that of Wordsworth. He is an elegant poet, primarily a maker rather than a "man speaking to men." His characteristic slow and stately cadence, his powerful rhythmic variation, as in the fourth line below, make the ballad something else again:

> Ah, what can ail thee, wretched wight,
>   Alone and palely loitering;
> The sedge is wither'd from the lake,
>   And no birds sing.

The ballad quality here is part of the attempt to recall a past age and through it achieve a sort of aesthetic distance. This is true to a certain extent also of Coleridge's "Ancient Mariner." Through several revisions Coleridge purged his poem of much archaic language and gave it a sophistication of diction that separates it from the popular ballad. Nevertheless, its balladic qualities are clear, and Coleridge's dissatisfaction with the "obtrusion of the moral sentiment so openly upon the reader" may have come as much from his feeling that he had violated balladic objectivity as from his belief that a poem should be concerned with the beautiful more than with discursive teaching.[8]

Rossetti's ballads in the mid-nineteenth century exist as evidence of the Pre-Raphaelite interest in things medieval. They have something in common with those of Keats in that they are very self-conscious in attention to rhythmic detail and to imagery. Rossetti's profusion of sensuous imagery suggests that he was more interested in the scene than the act, and in this he runs counter to the method of the popular ballad. "The Blessed Damozel" and "My Sister's Sleep" illustrate a descriptive interest not unnatural to a poet who was also a distinguished painter.

The balladeer's objectivity, somewhat lost in the intrusion of Wordsworth's speaker, is a means of expressing irony. Wordsworth's contemporary, William Blake, was one of the first to recognize this in his ironic ballads written in the Pickering manuscript, where the speaker drops the invective of some of the *Songs of Experience* and views the natural world from outside or above it. Extended use of the ironic potentiality of the ballad has been made by twentieth-century poets in an age where irony is a stock in poetic trade. Before examples, some definitions are in order. The usual twofold definition of irony as irony of statement (saying one thing and meaning another, usually its opposite) and irony of situation (a turn of events unexpected by the characters in a story but nearly inevitable to a detached observer) is not completely adequate. Irony can also be defined historically as a literary phase following upon the age of literary realism. It involves a vision of human limitation (and is thus associated with what T. E. Hulme and many modern writers have called "classicism") either cosmically

[8] *Selected Poetry and Prose*, p. 462.

necessary or comically stupid (as in satire). In any case the ironic poet makes a completely objective surface gesture, wears a mask. With it he observes a life worthy only of comic disdain or of a detachment which allows the devastating facts to speak for themselves.

It can be said, I suppose, that such detachment can be a form of understatement, often contrived to avoid an excess of sentiment (you can go too far in this direction and become sentimental again, as happens in much of Hemingway). One of the masters of the ironic ballad is W. H. Auden, among whose best known poems in this vein are "As I Walked Out One Evening" and "Let Me Tell You a Little Story," which is written to the tune of "St. James Infirmary." "Let Me Tell You . . ." speaks of a pathetic spinster who dies of cancer after a lifetime devoted to the protection of her virginity. After her death her body is dissected by medical students. Auden does not openly obtrude his moral — in fact, he never states it at all, but the sense of the poem is there in the total action. In another poem called "Victor Was a Little Baby," written to the tune of "Frankie and Johnny," Auden tells of jealousy between lovers in a story with all the trappings of modern psychology. Young Victor, brought up to avoid the plague of sin and without experience in love, marries a woman of low reputation, and discovers her past by overhearing his colleagues at the bank gossiping:

> Victor stood still as a statue,
>   The door was just ajar:
> One said; "God, what fun I had with her
>   In that Baby Austin car."
>
>   .   .   .   .   .   .
>
> Victor looked up at the sunset
>   As he stood there all alone;
> Cried; "Are you in Heaven, Father?"
>   But the sky said "Address not known."

The mountains, rivers, and trees, however, tell him to kill her. And he does so — with a carving knife. We last see poor Victor in an insane asylum making dolls out of clay and saying:

> . . . "I am Alpha and Omega, I shall come
>   To judge the earth one day."

These poems are brutally comic, while on the surface their attitudes are very detached.

Comic objectivity often turns upon the use of a cliché in some
unexpected way (as in Auden's line "address not known"), in a
sudden elegance or shift from the normal word order, often in the
use of outrageous surprise. Peter Miller's "The Capture of Edwin
Alonzo Boyd," based upon the capture of a famous criminal in
Toronto in 1953, displays the first and second qualities mentioned
above in a single line. As the cops sneak up on Boyd's hideout,

> When they saw him go in the cops radioed
>   to their Chief, "The Big Boy's here!",
> And the squad cars moved in silently
>   and grim was the atmosphere.

I refer, of course, to the last line, a "poetic" distortion of the normal word order and of newspaperese.

Surprise is the comic effect in this stanza:

> There was $25,000 in cash
>   in a briefcase by the bed,
> And a loaded pistol was in it too,
>   but Ed reached for his pants instead.

Boyd was captured in bed with his wife.

Understatement heightened by an internal rime yields comedy:

> And as Edwin Boyd, who was damned annoyed,
>   put his city clothes back on
> A committee waited down the stairs
>   to welcome him back to the Don.

Finally Boyd's bravado, expressed in an irony of statement, brings
the poem to an end. The mayor speaks:

> "You can be thankful you're alive," added he,
>   "and, not torn apart by a mob."
> "Why, yes," said Boyd with a gracious bow,
>   "You fellows did a fine job!"

These ballads of Auden and Miller are spare in sensuous description and sophisticated in wit. Poems approaching the ballad form
do so in a variety of ways. A narrative poem in quatrains which
observes a certain degree of detachment inevitably suggests the
ballad and calls for a traditional response on the reader's part. One
of the best poems of this sort in our time calls to mind a world of
chivalry and questing heroes pathetically unlike that of medieval
romance. John Crowe Ransom's Captain Carpenter, hero of the
poem named for him, is a worthy gentleman born into a world of
ironic realism rather than romance. His world is in one sense below him, but this fact, rather than working to his advantage, spells
his constant defeat. It is the kind of world he did not make. True
chivalry is dead, and he is even more pathetic than Don Quixote.
Nothing stops him from holding to his code until he is made to
suffer the final indignity.

Captain Carpenter rose up in his prime
Put on his pistols and went riding out
But had got wellnigh nowhere at that time
Till he fell in with ladies in a rout.

It was a pretty lady and all her train   5
That played with him so sweetly but before
An hour she'd taken a sword with all her main
And twined him of his nose for evermore.

Captain Carpenter mounted up one day
And rode straightway into a stranger rogue   10
That looked unchristian but be that as may
The Captain did not wait upon prologue.

But drew upon him out of his great heart
The other swung against him with a club
And cracked his two legs at the shinny part   15
And let him roll and stick like any tub.

Captain Carpenter rode many a time
From male and female took he sundry harms
He met the wife of Satan crying "I'm
The she-wolf bids you shall bear no more arms."   20

Their strokes and counters whistled in the wind
I wish he had delivered half his blows
But where she should have made off like a hind
The bitch bit off his arms at the elbows.

And Captain Carpenter parted with his ears 25
To a black devil that used him in this wise
O Jesus ere his threescore and ten years
Another had plucked out his sweet blue eyes.

Captain Carpenter got up on his roan
And sallied from the gate in hell's despite 30
I heard him asking in the grimmest tone
If any enemy yet there was to fight?

"To any adversary it is fame
If he risk to be wounded by my tongue
Or burnt in two beneath my red heart's flame 35
Such are the perils he is cast among.

"But if he can he has a pretty choice
From an anatomy with little to lose
Whether he cut my tongue and take my voice
Or whether it be my round red heart he choose." 40

It was the neatest knave that ever was seen
Stepping in perfume from his lady's bower
Who at this word put in his merry mien
And fell on Captain Carpenter like a tower.

I would not knock old fellows in the dust 45
But there lay Captain Carpenter on his back
His weapons were the old heart in his bust
And a blade shook between rotten teeth alack.

The rogue in scarlet and grey soon knew his mind
He wished to get his trophy and depart 50
With gentle apology and touch refined
He pierced him and produced the Captain's heart.

God's mercy rest on Captain Carpenter now
I thought him Sirs an honest gentleman
Citizen husband soldier and scholar enow 55
Let jangling kites eat of him if they can.

But God's deep curses follow after those
That shore him of his goodly nose and ears

His legs and strong arms at the two elbows
And eyes that had not watered seventy years.   60

The curse of hell upon the sleek upstart
That got the Captain finally on his back
And took the red red vitals of his heart
And made the kites to whet their beaks clack clack.[9]

It is unfortunately true that the good Captain is a bit of a fool
as well as an anachronism. Ransom's storyteller takes a friendly
attitude toward his hero, but he cannot mask the Captain's curious
combination of gallantry and stupidity which the telling of the
story inevitably must reveal. We are left teetering between affectionate respect and jeering disdain. Finally, the speaker, of course,
commits himself to an attitude, but it is more an attitude of rage
against the villain than approbation of the poor Captain. These
opposite attitudes are reflected in the curiously comical descriptions:

    And twined him of his nose for evermore,

or

    But where she should have made off like a hind
    The bitch bit off his arms at the elbows,

or

    From an anatomy with little to lose,

the last being a plain "gag," where a cliché is given a literal context.

Between the sophistication of this poem and the typical popular
ballad there is a considerable distance. But the simplicity of the
latter acts as a buffer against which the sophisticated poet can work
his ironies. In the contemporary poet's use of balladic form extremes meet; as Blake said, "Without contraries is no progression."

[9] Something might be said here of the punctuation of this poem and poems in
general. It is well to begin by remembering that punctuation was not always
codified among the educated as it is today. Furthermore, poets have always
used punctuation instead of letting it use them. The basic rhythmic units of
Ransom's poem are the line and the stanza. There is naturally a pause, however slight, at the end of each line. Ransom does not clutter his poem and over-
emphasize the pauses at the end of the lines by marks which would slow down
each stanza's thrust. In other words, the poet punctuates or does not punctuate
in order to set the rhythmic flow.

VI

We can all probably agree that today's popular songs are pretty much devoid of poetic merit. It is unlikely that any of them will appear in future anthologies of poetry. This has not always been the case. Some of the poems we now value highly were written as songs, and they were public in that they spoke of fundamental situations and passions: love, religion, loneliness, and simple enjoyment — as in, respectively, "Whoso that will" by King Henry VIII, "I sing of a maiden," "Western wind, when wilt thou blow," and "Jolly good ale and old." All of these poems are early songs. All of them except King Henry's are anonymous. Known later writers continued the tradition. One of these was, of course, Shakespeare, whose plays contained lyrics which became popular. A well known song is the following from *As You Like It* (V, iii):

> It was a lover and his lass,
>   With a hey, and a ho, and a hey nonino!
> That o'er the green cornfields did pass
> In the spring time, the only pretty ring time,
> When birds do sing hey ding a ding ding: 5
>   Sweet lovers love the Spring.
>
> Between the acres of the rye
> These pretty country folk would lie:
> This carol they began that hour,
> How that a life was but a flower.   10
>
> And therefore take the present time
>   With a hey, and a ho, and a hey nonino!
> For love is crowned with the prime
> In spring time, the only pretty ring time,
> When birds do sing hey ding a ding ding: 15
>   Sweet lovers love the Spring.

The popular song presents actions (if it presents them at all) for the sake of the feelings, but these feelings are not the poet's. The author disappears behind his song, and the feeling is common and identifiable as joy, grief, nostalgia, hope, prayer, etc. That Shakespeare's poem stands in a tradition of popular song is perhaps shown by the fact that early in the forties Bob Crosby's band set it to Dixieland.

In English poetry there is an unbroken lyric tradition, but after the eighteenth century the songs were rarely sung. One can follow the lyric from its anonymous beginnings through Wyatt, Sidney, Spenser, Shakespeare, the Cavalier Poets (Jonson's "Drink to Me Only with Thine Eyes," for example), Dryden, Gay's "Beggar's Opera," to Burns. But after Burns the song and the lyric poem are really two different things. There is nothing in modern popular music like Dryden's elegant "Song of Venus" or even Burns' "My Luve's Like a Red, Red Rose." With Blake we see the lyric turn symbolic and intellectual. Meanwhile the popular song has become mass-produced for public consumption. In recent years the writers and distributors have become aware that their greatest market is among adolescents. With this discovery the popular song has achieved a mediocrity never before approached. We seldom, if ever, find a popular song today with the grace and wit of Shakespeare's or Dryden's. Only jazz lyrics are of much interest, and there the human voice is a kind of musical instrument. The words themselves are less important than the rendition given them. Often a jazz singer will work with lyrics whose bare statement is sentimental. The singer's rendition will be calculated to destroy the sentimentality and actually mock the song's silliness, as in Louis Armstrong's "Blueberry Hill" or Fats Waller's "Up Jumped You with Love." Sometimes the song itself will contain this mockery of sentiment, as in the tune "Ugly Chile." A 1943 rendition by the sand-throated trombonist George Brunis is a classic of its sort:

> Aw
> You so ugly,
> You so ugly,
> You some ugly chile.
> Now the clothes that you wear are not in style;
> You look like un ape every time you smile.
> Oh how I hate you

5

You alligator bait you
The homeliest thing I ever saw.
You knock-kneed, pigeon-toed, box-ankled too,   10
There's a curse on your family and a spell on you.
Your hair is nappy.
Who's your pappy?
You some ugly chile.

You five by five and double-jointed too.   15
There's a curse on your family and it fell on you.
Your teeth are yella, who's your fella?
You some ugly chile.

The speaker's attitude toward this particular kind of ugliness changes. He moves from recognition through resentment to acceptance. In the first three lines he is incredulous, dumbfounded by the truth his own statement has revealed to him. "This," he seems to say, "is no joke." With recognition comes a burgeoning sense of outrage. His ego is profoundly abused. What follows is an indictment by catalogue. As he piles up evidence his sense of the fact's unacceptability grows, parallel with an awareness that this ugliness is not just notable, but practically unique. At the end of the catalogue he reaches the meaning of what he has revealed to himself. This is "the homeliest thing I ever saw." Yet even as he shows himself that the fact is even worse than it appeared at first sight, the fact becomes less unbearable. At this point in the lyric one misses the music: the parallel indictments — "knock-kneed, pigeon-toed," etc. — are made to pile up by a repeated two-note figure fitted to chords which demand resolution more intensely the oftener they are repeated. And the resolution comes in a disclaimer of responsibility. This "chile," the speaker implies, is more than ugly. This "chile" is against nature. Magic is invoked; only something which has power over nature could have made it.

But reconciliation is already near. "Your hair is nappy" is not really an indictment, but an affectionate pat on the head. In the ironic "who's your pappy?" the speaker, recognizing the inadequacy of what he has said so far, returns to nature, to a simple joke about bastardy; and finally the lyric comes full circle in the words that began it, ending in affectionate acceptance. This is the way things are, and nothing *this* ugly can be tragic. "It's funny. The joke is on me, see?"

These songs, more specifically these *renditions*, are different from tin-pan alley popular tunes, and certainly they are different from the "songs" of contemporary poets. They demonstrate something, however, already evident in the modern use of ballad forms. The singer's method is ironic. Through detachment or innuendo he often says something the words baldly on the page were not intended to mean. The movement in our time from the sentimental "pop" tune to Louis Armstrong's "rending" it seems to parallel roughly the growing emphasis on irony in modern song and ballad.

VII

But the balladeer need not adopt the ironic methods of Auden. Is it not possible to write a ballad of heroic action or a song of praise today? Perhaps it is more difficult since man has come more and more to find the source of his allegiance only within himself. Nevertheless, the case of Yeats from his late sixties to his death at seventy-three is interesting. Having lived through the Irish turmoil of 1916, the civil war, and the Free State, he considered that he had known heroes; and his ballads are songs of glorification, serious, direct, complete with refrain:

> Some had no thought of victory
> But had gone out to die
> That Ireland's mind be greater,
> Her heart mount up on high;
> And yet who knows what's yet to come?
> For Patrick Pearse had said
> That in every generation
> Must Ireland's blood be shed.
> *From mountain to mountain ride the*
> *fierce horsemen.*

Some Suggested Reading

Child, F. J., *English and Scottish Popular Ballads*.

Friedman, Albert B., *The Ballad Revival; The Viking Book of Folk Ballads*.

Gerould, Gordon H., *The Ballad of Tradition*.

Graves, Robert, *The English Ballad; English and Scottish Ballads*.

Gummere, Francis B., *The Popular Ballad*.

Percy, Thomas, *Reliques of Ancient English Poetry*.

NOTE: I wish to thank Mr. Bruce R. Park for his permission to reprint in slightly different form a discussion of "Ugly Chile" which originally appeared in our article "The State of the Jazz Lyric," *Chicago Review* X, 3 (Autumn–Winter 1956), pp. 5–20.

3 Sonnet:

POEM AS ARTIFICE

Dominant forms: Italian and English. Sources in Italy: Dante and Petrarch. Early English practice: Wyatt and Surrey. Broadening of subject and technique: Donne and Milton. Romantic attitudes: Coleridge and Wordsworth. Later inventions: Hopkins, Rossetti, Yeats.

1

Our approach to poetry in this chapter is through verse form. Poets have always invented rime schemes and rhythmical patterns, varying in complication from the difficult sestina to the blank verse of Elizabethan drama. Though inexperienced readers and embryonic poets may think that such rigid forms as the sestina and the sonnet are too restrictive, each verse form in itself should be considered a means to complete expression. Form of this sort is not a prison but a vehicle by means of which effects can be obtained. This chapter employs the sonnet to demonstrate the usefulness of verse form.

A poem is an artifice. If the poet is a bard, a storyteller, a "man speaking to men," we must also grant that he is a maker, a designer. There is a sense in which the poet, after his job is completed, no longer figures even as the teller of the tale. The poem takes on its own life independent of the poet. It speaks out of its own form. A study of the sonnet, whose artificial qualities are obvious, should make this aspect of poetry clear.

The sonnet came into being in Italy sometime during the thirteenth century, the age of Dante Alighieri, and reached its greatest popularity there in the fourteenth century with Petrarch. It appeared and flowered in England in the sixteenth century. Sir Thomas Wyatt and Henry Howard, Earl of Surrey, were both accomplished sonneteers and translators of Petrarch. Later in the century Sir Philip Sidney, Samuel Daniel, Michael Drayton, and of course Edmund Spenser, as well as many lesser poets, wrote sonnets. Shakespeare's famous sonnets were published in 1609. The period from Wyatt to Shakespeare was undoubtedly the great age of the English sonnet.

The sonnet is a demanding form even in its modern variations,[1]

---

[1] Although I believe, as I asserted in the Preface, that matters of rhythmic analysis are better taken up in class orally, some definitions are probably in order here. *Metrical analysis* of poetry divides lines into four basic kinds of feet:

iamb, or iambic foot:

> I sum/mon up/ remem/brance of/ . . .

troche, or trochaic foot:

> Captain/ Carpen/ter . . .

anapest, or anapestic foot:

> Afar/ from our lawn/ and our lev/ee . . .

dactyl, or dactylic foot:

> Mary, Mary quite contrary/ how does your/ garden grow?

The number of feet in the line describe the line: *monometer* (one foot), *dimeter, trimeter, tetrameter, pentameter, hexameter,* etc. The usual English sonnet is composed of iambic pentameter. All poems, however, have variations from the dominant pattern (as in the dactyl of "Mary, Mary" above) and should not be forced into a sing-song rhythm unnatural to the statement. For this reason most poems are better analyzed not according to metrical feet but by noting the number of dominant accents per line and where they fall. This number may be constant, or the lines may alternate in number of accents, or there may be all sorts of variations.

We should begin by assuming that *all* speech is rhythmic, that no system of analysis is more than an abstraction imposed on the poem from without, that systems of analysis are useful only as *indications* of how to read.

where the old "rules" of order are not so strictly kept and each poet invents a few of his own. As originated in Italy, it was simply a poem of about fourteen lines, but in the hands of Dante and Petrarch it evolved a particular rime scheme, length, and metrical pattern. The so-called Italian or Petrarchan sonnet is a poem of fourteen lines in iambic pentameter with a rime scheme that divides into an octave and sestet. The octave's scheme is usually *abbaabba,* but there are many variations of the rimes in the sestet, *cdcdcd* being one of the most popular. The English or Shakespearean sonnet maintains the same metrical pattern and number of lines but changes the rime scheme to *ababcdcdefefgg.* In spite of Shakespeare's consistent use of this pattern and an occasional adoption of it by Surrey and others, the Italian form has been the dominant one, even in English. During the sixteenth century and occasionally to this day, sonnets have been written in so-called sequences, or groups tied together usually by theme and mood. Though often the sonnets of a sequence appear to have a narrative framework, they seldom have primarily a narrative purpose and are more than likely symphonic in their development, passing through a series of meditations, presenting themes and variations.

The sixteenth-century sonneteers, influenced by the Italian tradition of Dante, Petrarch, and others, wrote almost invariably on the subject of love; and a certain number of set love situations began to appear. These in turn gave rise to conventional figures upon which the poets hung variation after variation. Because the sonnet is usually meditative in nature, the speaker makes an analysis of his love situation, often in the guise of an address to the beloved. In Shakespeare we see a certain enlargement of the number of subjects for meditation: death and lasting fame, the poet's own art, friendship, mutability — all interweaving with the love theme. Appearing after Shakespeare's, the sonnets of John Donne are all religious in subject, but some of the love conventions remain. God is now the desperately sought beloved. The speaker casts himself in the feminine, passive role, however. From Donne on, the subject matter of the sonnet broadens considerably, and at the same time the sonnet ceases to be primarily meditative in tone.

Milton is often declamatory; Meredith, detached and psychological as well as meditative.

   Of the two dominant kinds of sonnets each has its own particular
qualities. The younger form, the Shakespearean, is simpler, less
flexible, and more obvious in its possible uses than the Italian. Its
greatest strength is its capacity to suggest an inevitable movement
as if it were a logical argument toward a last witty couplet, which
drives down the point of the whole poem. Shakespeare's famous
sonnet XXX is a good example:

> When to the sessions of sweet silent thought
> I summon up remembrance of things past,
> I sigh the lack of many a thing I sought,
> And with old woes new wail my dear time's waste:
> Then can I drown an eye, unus'd to flow,   5
> For precious friends hid in death's dateless night,
> And weep afresh love's long-since-cancell'd woe,
> And moan th' expense of many a vanish'd sight:
> Then can I grieve at grievances foregone,
> And heavily from woe to woe tell o'er   10
> The sad account of fore-bemoanèd moan,
> Which I new pay as if not paid before.
>   But if the while I think on thee, dear friend,
>   All losses are restor'd and sorrows end.

The first quatrain sets the scene and situation with imagery of law
courts — "sessions" and "summon" — which lends dignity and for-
mality to the speaker's actions. The second quatrain, related to the
first by "then," which suggests a logical progression as well as a
temporal one, develops imagery of commerce in "cancell'd" and
"expense," and enlarges on the specific feelings of loss which the
speaker experiences. This sequence reaches its climax in the third
quatrain, where now because of the building-up of grief and the
repetition the poem demands relief. Finally there comes the epigrammatic twist of the couplet, which from the word "but" re-
laxes the tension and resolves the situation by completing the
monetary image. All losses are restored.

   The sonnet is very neatly organized according to a typical

Shakespearean pattern. Within it the poet can develop an image pattern, extend a metaphor, or rotate several metaphors, each fitting in its own quatrain, around a central theme. He can, of course, in order to establish his tone, heavily emphasize sound: "And with old woes new wail my dear time's waste," where alliteration, assonance, and a profusion of single-syllable words give weight and sinuousness to the expression. This line knocks against and demands release from the usual iambic pentameter line, which, when we read a sonnet, beats in the back of our brain. Shakespeare's line does not violate the established sonnet rhythmic pattern but works within it for its effects. As I. A. Richards has written, rhythm is established so that the poem can effect surprise and even betrayal. This is one of the purposes of artifice.

Nor does Shakespeare violate the typical sonnet rime pattern. It is easy to see that in many of his sonnets Shakespeare is quite content with three quatrains which lend the sense of an argument developed logically, building toward an inevitable resolution. The effect is most often one of stateliness, an evenness of tone which suggests a thoughtful speaker adequately detached from sentimentality, detached enough that he can employ the hyperbole of the drowned eye without the reader's feeling excess. This is not to say that all of Shakespeare's sonnets have the same tone (witness the one beginning "The expense of spirit . . .") but that the dominating quality is one of meditative detachment and serious wit.

The sonnet (CXLVI) below develops a similar pattern of imagery. The dialogue of the self and soul is not an unusual poetic form. Here the poet does not allow the soul to reply but spins the answers out of his own questions. The quatrains are not so clearly divided, the argument consisting of a building-up of questions, and the turnabout occurring in line 9 with the couplet as a conclusion to the poet's advice:

> Poor soul, the center of my sinful earth,
> Leagued with these rebel powers that thee array,[2]

[2] "Leagued with" is an editor's invention to cover a printer's error in the original edition.

Why dost thou pine within and suffer dearth,
Painting thy outward walls so costly gay?
Why so large cost, having so short a lease,   5
Dost thou upon thy fading mansion spend?
Shall worms, inheritors of this excess,
Eat up thy charge? is this thy body's end?
Then, soul, live thou upon thy servant's loss,
And let that pine to aggravate thy store;   10
Buy terms divine in selling hours of dross;
Within be fed, without be rich no more:
    So shalt thou feed on Death, that feeds on men,
    And Death once dead, there's no more dying then.

This poem divides itself at the point which would normally divide octave and sestet in the Italian sonnet. And it is somewhat Italian in structure, if still Shakespearean in its witty closing couplet.

The Italian form, as is perhaps indicated by Shakespeare's sliding over toward its divisions above, has more various uses. There are two larger units of statement. There is the possibility of a turn of thought at line 9. The couplet can be maintained at the end of the sestet or not, according to the demands of the poem. The Italian sonnet seems better adapted to the description of action, with the octave setting the scene and leading up to the climax in the sestet, as in Sonnet I of Rossetti's "Willowwood":

I sat with love upon a woodside well,
    Leaning across the water, I and he;
    Nor ever did he speak nor looked at me,
But touched his lute wherein was audible
The certain secret thing he had to tell: 5
    Only our mirrored eyes met silently
    In the low wave; and that sound came to be
The passionate voice I knew; and my tears fell.

And at their fall, his eyes beneath grew hers;
And with his foot and with his wing-feathers   10
    He swept the spring that watered my heart's drouth.
Then the dark ripples spread to waving hair,
And as I stooped, her own lips rising there
    Bubbled with brimming kisses at my mouth.

The poet makes full use of the break after the octave, at which point the action has been arrested and we stand on the brink of a new development. Inside line 8 there is a pause, and the line levels out in words of one syllable, each of which has about the same weight of accent. We stop and allow ourselves to contemplate the arrested scene. The two are looking at each other's reflections in the water, stilled almost to garden statuary. Then the sestet, in a kind of repetition, mentions the tears falling, and we are plunged into the climax. The arrested action is disturbed just as the water is, and the final action of love and the clouded image reflect the speaker's psychological state. I have always been particularly pleased by the slight ruffling of the rhythm in "wing-feathers" (line 10), an effect typical of Rossetti's delicate technique.

11

Rossetti, a nineteenth-century English poet born of Italian parents and schooled in Italian literary traditions, returned to some of the conventions of the renaissance sonnet. We can see this in "Willow-wood" and in the subject matter itself. He was greatly influenced by Dante, and in particular by Dante's *Vita Nuova*, which he translated. The *Vita Nuova* is a sonnet sequence strung together with prose transitions, and explications of the sonnets. The subject is the poet's love for the beautiful Beatrice, whose death first causes sorrow and then spiritual elevation. Here from the *Vita Nuova* is a prose passage and the sonnet that follows it. The translation is Rossetti's:

> . . . It chanced on a day that my most gracious lady was with a gathering of ladies in a certain place; to the which I was conducted by a friend of mine; he thinking to do me a great pleasure by showing me the beauty of so many women. Then I, hardly knowing whereunto he conducted me, but trusting in him (who yet was leading his friend to the last verge of life), made questions: "To what end are we come among these ladies?" and he answered: "To the end that they may be worthily served." And they were assembled around a gentlewoman who was given in marriage on that day; the custom of the city being that these

should bear her company when she sat down for the first time at table in the house of her husband. Therefore I, as was my friend's pleasure, resolved to stay with him and do honour to those ladies. But as soon as I had thus resolved, I began to feel a faintness and a throbbing at my left side, which soon took possession of my whole body. Whereupon I remember that I covertly leaned my back unto a painting that ran around the walls of that house; and being fearful that my trembling should be discerned of them, I lifted mine eyes to look on those ladies, and then first perceived among them the excellent Beatrice. And when I perceived her, all my senses were overpowered by the great lordship that Love obtained, finding him so near unto that most gracious being until nothing but the spirits of sight remained to me; and even these remained driven out of their own instruments because Love entered into that honoured place of theirs, so that he might better behold her. And although I was other than at first, I grieved for the spirits so expelled which kept up a sore lament, saying: "If he had not in this wise thrust us forth, we should also behold the marvel of this lady." By this, many of her friends, having discerned my confusion, began to wonder; and together with herself, kept whispering of me and mocking me. Whereupon my friend, who knew not what to conceive, took me by the hands, and drawing me forth from among them, required to know what ailed me. Then, having first held me at quiet for a space until my perceptions were come back to me, I made answer to my friend: "Of a surety I have now set my feet on that point of life, beyond the which he must not pass who would return." Afterwards, leaving him, I went back to the room where I had wept before; and again weeping and ashamed, said: "If this lady but knew of my condition, I do not think that she would thus mock at me; nay, I am sure that she must needs feel some pity." And in my weeping I bethought me to write certain words in the which, speaking to her, I should signify the occasion of my disfigurement, telling her also how I knew that she had no knowledge thereof: which, if it were known, I was certain must move others to pity. And then, because I hoped that peradventure it might come into her hearing, I wrote this sonnet:

> Even as the others mock, thou mockest me;
>   Not dreaming, noble lady, whence it is
>   That I am taken with strange semblances,
>   Seeing thy face which is so fair to see:

For else, compassion would not suffer thee   5
   To grieve my heart with such harsh scoffs as these.
   Lo! Love, when thou art present, sits at ease,
   And bears his mastership so mightily,
That all my troubled senses he thrusts out,
   Sorely tormenting some, and slaying some,   10
   Till none but he is left and has free range
To gaze on thee. This makes my face to change
   Into another's; while I stand all dumb,
   And hear my senses clamour in their rout.

The prose here seems at first glance more important than the sonnet. It tells the story. Each sonnet in the sequence, however, fixes
a situation which transcends the narrative surrounding it. Dante's
sonnet above is concerned primarily with the psychological condition which the situation calls forth, secondarily with praise of a
beloved whose simple presence can bring about such a condition.
The narrative piece is in a way a long footnote, something like part
of a literary biography written to help us understand a poet's work
more fully. Dante the prose writer acts the part of a Dante scholar.
The situation of importance is *in* the sonnet and is only super-
ficially *described* in the prose. Later poets cease to be their own
commentators and leave the sonnet sequence free of prose inter-
ludes.

The central figure employed in this poem, the personification of
love, is a convention among renaissance sonneteers. It is in Petrarch, from whom it came into England through Wyatt and Surrey. It can be tedious like any well-known and well-worn device,
but a good sonneteer does something with it, as Dante does here.
He makes it work to establish the speaker's state. The personification of love succeeds not merely in giving "love" importance but
in assigning it a certain kind of power: "Love, when thou art present, sits at ease." Love has considerable self-confidence and even
insolence in the face of the speaker's obvious desire to maintain a
decorous outward manner before his lady. Love plays the tyrant
with the lover's senses, destroying and tormenting at will; for love
seeks to achieve his impertinent desire. The speaker thinks this an

unflattering lasciviousness and is tormented by his inability to control the expression of his love. He is sorely embarrassed; he cannot hold back his emotions; he is finally left dumb. Love triumphs over his reason, and in an image of a routed army in disorganized retreat, the power of speech is also routed. This last image, which brings the poem to a close, seems to me very powerful in its evocation of the chaos into which the speaker's emotions have been hurled.

Petrarch's sonnets had a greater influence on sixteenth-century English poetry than did Dante's. The two poems below are translations by Wyatt and Surrey of one of Petrarch's sonnets:

> The long love that in my thought I harbor,
> And in my heart doth keep his residence,
> Into my face presseth with bold pretense
> And there campeth, displaying his banner.
> She that me learns to love and to suffer   5
> And wills that my trust and lust's negligence
> Be reigned with reason, shame, and reverence,
> With his hardiness takes displeasure.
> Wherewith love to the heart's forest he fleeth,
> Leaving his enterprise with pain and cry,   10
> And there him hideth, and not appeareth:
> What may I do when my master feareth
> But in the field with him to live and die?
> For good is the life ending faithfully.
>
>   (Wyatt)

> Love that liveth and reigneth in my thought,
> That built his seat within my captive breast,
> Clad in the arms wherein with me he fought,
> Oft in my face he doth his banner rest.
> She that me taught to love and suffer pain,   5
> My doubtful hope and eke my hot desire
> With shamefast cloak to shadow and refrain,
> Her smiling grace converteth straight to ire;
> And coward love then to the heart apace
> Taketh his flight, whereas he lurks and plains   10
> His purpose lost, and dare not show his face.
> For my lord's guilt thus faultless bide I pains;

Yet from my lord shall not my foot remove, —
Sweet is his death that takes his end by love.

(Surrey)

Wyatt's poem is clearly much "rougher" in its rhythms and more
varied in its rimes. It gives the effect of a more "natural" statement.
In contrast, Surrey's poem is reserved, "smoother," metronomic.
Surrey's poem keeps its distance, is more aloof from the reader
than Wyatt's. As the sonnet developed after Shakespeare it was
the "natural" language of Wyatt that seemed to gain domination.
But in the sixteenth century Surrey's tone is closer to the main
stream of the form, as exemplified by Spenser, Daniel, and Shakespeare.

Wyatt's poem contains effects that appeal to the modern ear.
I, for one, have always been much attracted by his first line. The
unusual use of the adjective "long" and its alliteration with "love"
seems deliberately suggestive of the speaker's emotion, a quality
I shall not attempt to translate into other terms. This emotion is
"harbored" in the speaker's "thought." The image expresses the
very delicate nature of the speaker's feelings. The speaker admits
a willing restraint and shyness, a gallant decorum in his relations
with the lady, which she not only demands but he also accepts as
proper and to be desired. It is a very dignified image, unobtrusive
and conventional enough not to overstate itself and spoil the effect
in sentimentality. The image is immediately thrown into sharp
contrast with the state of affairs that succeeds it. Now love, which
as in Dante is the passions, becomes bold, destroys the courtier-like
restraint with which the speaker has harbored his love. The succeed-
ing image has a touch of impudence about it. Love is the villainous
knight, who shows himself freely in the face of the "enemy" without stealth but boldly as if to challenge. Tremendous rhythmic
variations, the feminine endings of the enclosing rimes,[3] and the
use of inner off-rimes (face–presseth, presseth–campeth) all con-

[3] Feminine endings are those that conclude lines on an unaccented syllable.
In this poem I refer particularly to "harbor," "banner," "suffer," and "dis-
pleasure."

tribute to the quality of the octave. The complex interlocking sounds contribute (I am unprepared to say quite how) to breaking down the distance between the speaker and the reader. The continuation of feminine endings in the second quatrain gives an abruptness to each line; and this, in conflict with the run-on nature of the lines, makes the mistress' actions seem hard and cold, the speaker's situation painful. The poem ends in a curious way, on a dying note. Certainly the last line, with its weak last syllable and rime, is unpretentious, nearly anticlimactic, though rightly so, and suggestive of a difficult acceptance willingly made. The speaker has really disapproved of love's action, has desired restraint and dignity. Yet love does express his true feelings. Caught in this conflict he acts the faithful vassal. Now that love has expressed itself as it has he cannot deny it, for that would be hypocritical and "untrue" both to his feelings and to his lady, even if she disapproves.

Surrey's sonnet has a totally different tone. Even details of the action are significantly changed. The rhythm is more metronomic, the sound structure less eccentric. Surrey's strategy is to generalize the situation. While Wyatt writes only about one occurrence when love emerged into the speaker's face, Surrey asserts that this has often happened and generalizes from it. The speaker's struggle is made somewhat less immediate by our knowing that it has occurred several times before. Everything is put a bit more baldly in Surrey's version. Speaker and love fight with each other; the shamefulness of desire is emphasized; love is described as cowardly and acts almost absurdly when finally he is routed. The sonnet is Shakespearean and ends in a couplet, yet the couplet is not, I think, successful: line 13 can be read to produce a ludicrous image, and the poet is forced to use a rather weak metaphor for death ("end") in order to complete his epigrammatic last line. It seems to me that Wyatt's dramatic immediacy, his "roughness," his more restrained descriptions, and his conclusion make his translation preferable *as a poem*, if not necessarily as a translation of Petrarch.

But Surrey's poem does not fairly represent the "smooth" sixteenth-century sonnet. Something by Spenser may better illustrate the power of the more conventional methods. Spenser is by comparison to Wyatt an elegant poet, and by comparison to Surrey simply a better sonneteer at a similar game. There is often in Spenser the same detached manner, an almost aloof tone. One figure is developed fully through the poem, and this single emphasis may contribute to the sense of detachment from the reader. A sonnet of such quality is number XI of the *Amoretti*, but number X interests me more for what Rosemond Tuve has called its "tone of delicate mockery" to which conventional images puffed up to express the poet's attitude contribute.[4] The "huge massacres" of line 6 below is such a tremendous hyperbole that the statement can only be taken as ironic. The poet is aware of his own exasperation and is willing to laugh at it while excoriating the mistress for causing him such difficulties. The hyperbole is at the center of this feeling.

> Unrighteous Lord of Love, what law is this,
> That me thou makest thus tormented be,
> The whiles she lordeth in licentious blisse
> Of her freewill, scorning both thee and me?
> See how the tyrannesse doth joy to see   5
> The huge massacres which her eyes do make,
> And humbled harts brings captive unto thee,
> That thou of them mayst mightie vengeance take!
> But her proud hart doe thou a little shake,
> And that high look, with which she doth comptroll   10
> All this world's pride, bow to a baser make,
> And al her faults in thy black booke enroll:
> That I may laugh at her in equall sort
> As she doth laugh at me, and makes my pain her sport.[5]

Shakespeare, too, stands in the line of "smoothness." He is more like Surrey than Wyatt, though different in mood from all that precede him. Shakespeare can, in one instance, make violent fun of the conventional love sonnet, which by his time has worn out its descriptions of the lovely mistress. Something of the difference

---

[4] *Elizabethan and Metaphysical Imagery*, Chicago, 1961, p. 64.
[5] This line, which is elongated from the dominant iambic pentameter to hexameter, is called an *alexandrine*.

in temper between Shakespeare and Sidney can be seen in the way
they joke with the conventions, Sidney gently and Shakespeare a
bit more raucously. First Sidney:

> Some lovers speak, when they their muses entertain,
>> Of hopes begot by fear, of wot not what desires,
>> Of force of heav'nly beams infusing hellish pain,
>> Of living deaths, dear wounds, fair storms, and freezing
>>> fires;
> Someone his song in Jove and Jove's strange tales attires, 5
>> Bordered with bulls and swans, powdered with golden rain;
>> Another humbler wit to shepherd's pipe retires,
>> Yet hiding royal blood full oft in rural vein;
> To some a sweetest plaint a sweetest style affords,
>> While tears pour out his ink, and sighs breathe out
>>> his words, 10
>> His paper pale despair, and pain his pen doth move.
> I can speak what I feel, and feel as much as they,
>> But think that all the map of my state I display
>> When trembling voice brings forth that I do Stella love.

This sonnet, written in alexandrines instead of the more traditional
pentameter, is a good-natured spoof at the conventions of the love
sonnet once they get out of hand. It is certainly true that the sonnet from Dante and Petrarch made much of hyperbolic extended
figures. Love affairs were treated in titanic terms (without the irony
of Spenser's "massacres") or by a minute analysis of the physical
debilitation of the lover in a state of hopeless desire. What Sidney
does here, of course, is to hold for "sincerity," but not too seriously; for he already knows that sincerity is also a convention. His
line is to parade his own incompetence, his inarticulate state. But,
of course, he knows, and the reader is supposed to know, that he
is not inarticulate, that his own poem proves him possessed of a
new eloquence. The statement is not then really sincere but "sincere" — a new and more complicated form of hyperbole. The tradition of a contest in hyperbole for the hand of the beloved is continued in a different guise.

Shakespeare takes a bolder tack:

My mistress' eyes are nothing like the sun;
Coral is far more red than her lips red;
If snow be white, why then her breasts are dun;
If hairs be wires, black wires grow on her head.
I have seen roses damask'd, red and white,   5
But no such roses see I in her cheeks;
And in some perfumes is there more delight
Than in the breath that from my mistress reeks.
I love to hear her speak, yet well I know
That music hath a far more pleasing sound;   10
I grant I never saw a goddess go;
My mistress when she walks, treads on the ground:
   And yet by heaven, I think my love as rare
   As any she belied with false compare.

Faced with this sonnet and Sidney's, we see that the poets are clearly more interested in *writing a sonnet* than in praising the lady. "Sincerity" is not really the standard but a kind of wit. The poets vie with conventions of statement, turn them upside down, mock them when they become clichés and are no longer capable of containing thought. Still, the conventions are not wholly rejected. Even at the end of his poem Shakespeare invokes heaven, asserts that if other poets were not to make false comparisons then indeed his lady would prove at once to outshine all others. In a word he is still within the love-sonnet tradition, but he has carried it well beyond Petrarch by inverting it. Even so, all conventions of this sort gradually work themselves out. The sonnet in Shakespeare's time was tied not so much to standard figures as to the subject of love (much as the popular song is now).

III

It is no surprise that after Sidney's gentle mockery and Shakespeare's foray a new note should creep in. The Petrarchan conventions of love praise were too deeply cracked to contain any longer the proper feelings. With a change in subject and attitude comes always a change in technique. The *Holy Sonnets* of John Donne are our next exhibit. Donne is "rough," but more self-consciously so than Wyatt. He is fond of run-on lines, puts less emphasis on the rimes, changes his pace (line 9), writes in a rhythm that takes careful liberties with the regular iambic (lines 6 and 7):

> At the round earths imagin'd corners, blow
> Your trumpets, Angels, and arise, arise
> From death, you numberless infinities
> Of soules, and to your scattred bodies goe,
> All whom the flood did, and fire shall o'erthrow,   5
> All whom warre, dearth, age, agues, tyrannies
> Despaire, law, chance, hath slaine, and you whose eyes
> Shall behold God, and never tast deaths woe.
> But let them sleepe, Lord, and mee mourne a space,
> For, if above all these, my sinnes abound,   10
> 'Tis late to aske abundance of thy grace,
> When wee are there; here on this lonely ground,
> Teach mee how to repent; for that's as good
> As if thou' hadst seal'd my pardon, with thy blood.
>
> *(Holy Sonnet VIII)*

One of the finest things about this sonnet is Donne's taking advantage of the natural pause and turnabout from octave to sestet. That change of pace, the total shift of mood from the violent marching beats of lines 5 to 8 to the tone of "But let them sleepe, Lord . . ." is one of the great *tours de force* in a sequence of sonnets which contain many startling effects.

The sonnet below (*Holy Sonnet II*) is perhaps more typical of Donne in subject matter:

> As due by many titles I resigne
> My selfe to thee, O God, first I was made
> By thee, and for thee, and when I was decay'd
> Thy blood bought that, the which before was thine;
> I am thy sonne, made with thy selfe to shine,   5
> Thy servant, whose paines thou hast still repaid,
> Thy sheepe, thine Image, and, till I betray'd
> My selfe, a temple of thy Spirit divine;
> Why dost the devill then usurpe on mee?
> Why doth he steale, nay ravish that's thy right?   10
> Except thou rise and for thine owne worke fight,

> O I shall soone despaire, when I doe see
> That thou lov'st mankind well, yet wilt'not chuse mee.
> And Satan hates mee, yet is loth to lose mee.

The pun on "son–sun" of line 5 and the piling-up of evidence leading to the double paradox of the final couplet are characteristic.
The subject is love, but that between man and God. The speaker
casts himself, if we are seeking an analogy to the Petrarchan sonnet, as the feminine figure. The imagery is now, however, Biblical.
The speaker has expended all his energies, waits for God to ravish
him and save him from the Devil. The poem has an urgency about
it not characteristic of love sonnets, partially because of the subject but also because of the technique. The speaker's violent spiritual state is reflected by the "roughness" of the poem, by the more
complex rhythm, the truncated lines, the imploring questions.

Donne's sonnets are not elegant or stately meditations or la-
ments. They are dramatic. The other great sonneteer of the seventeenth century, John Milton, is not like Donne; but one can see
that he too reflects a change from Elizabethan modes. His tone *is*
stately, his subject matter varied. If Donne gives us cacaphony, as
here (the opening lines of *Holy Sonnet XIV*),

> Batter my heart, three person'd God; for, you
> As yet but knocke, breathe, shine, and seeke to mend;
> That I may rise, and stand, o'erthrow mee, and bend
> Your force, to breake, blowe, burne, and make me new,

Milton is resonant. Vowels and rimes in "On the Late Massacre in
Piedmont" support the violence of the statement, but the effects remain below the surface swelling of a whole symphonic arrangement:

> Avenge, O Lord, thy slaughtered saints, whose bones
>   Lie scattered on the Alpine mountains cold;
>   Even them who kept thy truth so pure of old,
>   When all our fathers worshipped stocks and stones,
> Forget not: in thy book record their groans   5
>   Who were thy sheep, and in their ancient fold
>   Slain by the bloody Piemontese, that rolled

Mother with infant down the rocks. Their moans
The vales redoubled to the hills, and they
To Heaven. Their martyred blood and ashes sow   10
O'er all th' Italian fields, where still doth sway
The triple Tyrant; that from these may grow
A hundredfold, who, having learnt thy way,
Early, may fly the Babylonian woe.

Worth particular examination here are the riming words and the
play through them on "O." The old limitations of subject matter
are ignored: Milton's sonnets are almost all "occasional" pieces.
Even satire and invective are now apparently acceptable in the
sonnet. This gradual breakdown in the conventions of subject
matter must have raised questions about the whole point of the
form which grew up with those conventions. Between Milton and
Wordsworth there is no considerable sonneteer. The period
abounded in poems of heroic couplets, in the verse essay (see
Chapter 5), and in forms more suited to variety of subject. When
the Petrarchan sonnet conventions broke down, the sonnet, too,
for a time lost its popularity. When it regained its popularity not
only were the love conventions absent, but the poets also eman-
cipated themselves from strict adherence to the Italian or Shakespearean forms. The forms became loose containers which suggested rather than demanded a certain resolution. The sonnet's
artifice was now primarily evident in its diction and its daring
rhythmic variations.

IV

In the *Biographia Literaria*, Coleridge discusses the early influence
upon him of the sonnets of William Lisle Bowles. By 1800 Bowles
was already a somewhat old-fashioned poet, surely not one who
impresses us much today. But to Coleridge he conveyed the possibility of a new style, bringing together the head and heart. That
is the way Coleridge put it:

One great distinction, I appeared to myself to see plainly, between, even the characteristic faults of our elder poets, and the
false beauty of the moderns. In the former, from Donne to

Cowley, we find the most fantastic out-of-the-way thoughts, but in the most pure and genuine mother English; in the latter, the most obvious thoughts, in language the most fantastic and arbitrary. Our faulty elder poets sacrificed the passion and passionate flow of poetry, to the subtleties of intellect, and to the starts of wit; the moderns to the glare and glitter of a perpetual, yet broken and heterogeneous imagery, or rather to an amphibious something, made up, half of image, and half of abstract meaning. [Coleridge gives in a footnote, as an example, the following lines:

> No more will I endure love's pleasing pain,
> Or round my *heart's leg* tie his galling chain.]

The one sacrificed the heart to the head; the other both heart and head to point the drapery.

The reader must make himself acquainted with the general style of composition that was at that time deemed poetry, in order to understand and account for the effect produced on me by the Sonnets, the "Monody at Matlock" and the "Hope," of Mr. Bowles; for it is peculiar to original genius to become less and less *striking*, in proportion to its success in improving the taste and judgment of its contemporaries. . . . Whatever relation, therefore, of cause or impulse Percy's collection of Ballads may bear to the most *popular* poems of the present day; yet in a more sustained and elevated style, of the then living poets, Bowles and Cowper were, to the best of my knowledge, the first who combined natural thoughts with natural diction; the first who reconciled the heart with the head.[6]

We are inclined to agree with Coleridge's observation that Bowles' sonnets may not be particularly interesting to later readers. We see, as apparently Coleridge had begun to see, in "Hope" (below) the generalized, somewhat insipid language of the late eighteenth century. The danger for the follower of Milton was that he might exchange resonance for bombast. Bowles' language does at least reject the bombastic and purges itself of the worn-out mythological decoration popular in the earlier part of the century:

> As one who, long by wasting sickness worn,
> Weary has watched the lingering night, and heard
> Unmoved the carol of the matin bird

[6] *Selected Poetry and Prose*, pp. 198–199.

Salute his lonely porch; now first at morn
Goes forth, leaving his *melancholy bed;*   5
He the green slope and level meadow views,
Delightful bathed with slow-ascending dews;
Or marks the clouds, that o'er the mountain's head
In varying forms fantastic wander white;
Or turns his ear to every random song,   10
Heard the green river's winding marge along,
The while each sense is steeped in still delight.
So *o'er my breast young Summer's breath I feel,*
Sweet Hope! thy fragrance pure and healing incense steal!

The words in italics mark areas of the poem which do not utterly
reject the outworn phraseology. The first two are rather silly deco-
rative metaphors and the next-to-last line is a metaphor that gets
out of hand.

It was the poetry of Wordsworth that seems to fit Coleridge's
description better than Bowles'. In his famous *Preface* Wordsworth
held out for a revolution in poetic diction, scorning the "gaudiness
and inane phraseology of modern writers." Wordsworth takes one
of Gray's sonnets as an object for criticism:

> I will here adduce a short composition of Gray, who was at the
> head of those who, by their reasonings, have attempted to widen
> the space of separation betwixt prose and metrical composition,
> and was more than any other man curiously elaborate in the struc-
> ture of his own poetic diction:

In vain to me the smiling mornings shine,
And reddening Phoebus lifts his golden fire:
The birds in vain their amorous descant join,
Or cheerful fields resume their green attire.
These ears, alas! for other notes repine;
A different object do these eyes require;
My lonely anguish melts no heart but mine;
And in my breast the imperfect joys expire;
Yet morning smiles the busy race to cheer,
And new-born pleasure brings to happier men;
The fields to all their wonted tribute bear;
To warm their little loves the birds complain.

> *I fruitless mourn to him that cannot hear,*
> *And weep the more because I weep in vain.*

It will easily be perceived, that the only part of this sonnet which is of any value is the lines printed in italics; it is equally obvious that, except in the rhyme, and in the use of the single word "fruitless" for fruitlessly, which is so far a defect, the language of these lines does in no respect differ from that of prose.[7]

After Gray one of Wordsworth's poems does seem "prosaic," but he would have taken that as a compliment. He avoids the usual personifications (like that of the sun above); his language is comparatively simple and direct:

> Surprised by joy — impatient as the Wind
> I turned to share the transport — Oh! with whom
> But Thee, deep buried in the silent tomb,
> That spot which no vicissitude can find?
> Love, faithful love, recalled thee to my mind —   5
> But how could I forget thee? Through what power,
> Even for the least division of an hour,
> Have I been so beguiled as to be blind
> To my most grievous loss! — That thought's return
> Was the worst pang that sorrow ever bore,   10
> Save one, one only, when I stood forlorn,
> Knowing my heart's best treasure was no more;
> That neither present time, nor years unborn
> Could to my sight that heavenly face restore.

As we saw in the previous chapter, Wordsworth is fond of making a poem turn upon a dramatic moment in which things are suddenly seen in a new and curious perspective. Here the typical Wordsworthian illusion is not optical but the result of habit. The speaker by force of a very dear habit turns to speak to a person now dead, turning back the time in a moment of joy. He discovers, however, the black nothingness of his loss all over again. It is a powerful poem true to the poet's desire to make the situation and action expressive of feeling. In form it is a loose sonnet. There is no rigid adherence to the usual Italian divisions. The major breaks occur

---

[7] *The Prelude*, etc., pp. 10–11.

within the lines. The sonnet skeleton has receded somewhat behind the expression, yet it is apparent as a formalizing device.

This simplicity of language and unassuming opening of the speaker's heart was not as common prior to Wordsworth's poetic revolution, but it was not a monopoly of the romantic poets either. Witness the sonnet which Ezra Pound nominates as perhaps the most perfect in the language. It was written by a little known Scots poet, Mark Alexander Boyd (1563–1601):

> Fra bank to bank, fra wood to wood I rin
> Ourhailit with my feeble fantasie
> Like til a leaf that fallis from a tree
> Or til a reed ourblawin with the wind,
>
> Two gods guides me, the ane of them is blin,   5
> Yea, and a bairn brocht up in vanitie,
> The next a wife ingenrit of the sea
> And lichter nor a dauphin with her fin.
>
> Unhappy is the man for evermair
> That tills the sand and sawis in the air,   10
>
> But twice unhappier is he, I lairn,
> That feidis in his heart a mad desire
> And follows on a woman throw the fire
> Led by a blind and teachit by a bairn.[8]

In spite of the redundance of its last line, in which "blind" and "bairn" both refer to Cupid, this poem is to be admired for its effective simplicity of diction and syntax, its refusal to choose all of the elaborate poetic ways to appear dignified, its determination to keep to the immediate experience in every line. The poet chooses unobtrusive similes to describe his innocent helplessness. He is afraid neither to employ the proverb of lines 9 and 10 nor frankly admit a "mad desire" and say no more to embellish it. His blind irresponsible Cupid and the Venus whose loveliness is caught in one delicate metaphor do not have the quality of sheer decoration, like Gray's Phoebus.

[8] *ourhailit:* overcome, carried away; *blin:* blind; *wife:* woman; *ingenrit:* engendered; *lichter:* more capricious.

V

After Wordsworth, after Keats and his rich sensuousness (to be discussed later), the nineteenth century exhibits considerable variety among its sonneteers. There is the famous sonnet in alexandrines by Ernest Dowson called "To One in Bedlam," which begins with these fine lines:

> With delicate mad hands, behind his sordid bars,
> Surely he hath his posies, which they tear and twine.

There are the sixteen-line sonnets by George Meredith which form the sequence "Modern Love." There are the experiments in rhythm and image by Hopkins (including his ten-line sonnets). There is the return to certain Petrarchan conventions by Rossetti. An example of what the sonnet comes to contain is Hopkins' *tour de force*, "The Windhover," which has been much anthologized and discussed. Perhaps "Felix Randal" will serve as well:

> Felix Randal the farrier, O is he dead then? my duty
>   all ended,
> Who have watched his mould of man, big-boned and
>   hardy-handsome
> Pining, pining, till time when reason rambled in it
>   and some
> Fatal four disorders, fleshed there, all contended?
>
> Sickness broke him. Impatient he cursed at first,
>   but mended   5
> Being anointed and all; though a heavenlier heart
>   began some
> Months earlier, since I had our sweet reprieve and
>   ransom
> Tendered to him. Ah well, God rest him all road ever
>   he offended!
>
> This seeing the sick endears them to us, us too it
>   endears,
> My tongue had taught thee comfort, touch had quenched
>   thy tears,   10

Thy tears that touched my heart, child, Felix, poor
Felix Randal;

How far from then forethought of, all thy more
boisterous years,
When thou at the random grim forge, powerful amidst
peers,
Didst fettle for the great grey drayhorse his bright
and battering sandal!

The speaker is, of course, a priest. Let me observe that I have never read a Hopkins poem which did not seem to me to have some slight excess or failure of language. His weakness is usually an excessive striving to fill his poem to the brim with intensity. The alliteration of "powerful amidst peers" seems to me such an excess; it seems to be chosen at the expense of naturalness of statement. On the other hand there are few of his poems which I do not greatly admire. This one makes fine use of its form as it sways in tone through the various sonnet divisions. The change of pace characteristic of the Donne sonnet already quoted is here multiplied into a series of wave-like movements from description to impassioned comment. Note the break in pace between the second quatrain and the sestet, and how the sestet, beginning with that detached generalized observation, rises to the immediate hard, bright, glorious vision of the last line. Or note the sweeping movement of the feeling upward to line 3: "pining, pining"; and the jostling of words in line 4, as the whole quatrain breaks in the chaos of Felix Randal's four disorders.

Rossetti, who seems to me the other greatest (but also uneven) sonneteer of the period, is not as eccentric, as surprising as Hopkins, and never as compelling. Nevertheless he reflects an interest in the possibilities of rhythm straining against a tight demanding verse form. Rossetti's weakness is sentimentalism, which in his poems often expresses itself as a tendency toward an unrestrained cry of pain or passionate love. Songs of lost love, of course, are prone to this sort of trouble. The poem below, which runs the danger of sentimentality in its subject matter, succeeds in keeping

just this side of it. One of the reasons this poem is successful is that
it effectively exploits very intricate sound patterns:

> What of her glass without her? The blank gray
>   There where the pool is blind of the moon's face.
>   Her dress without her? The tossed empty space
> Of cloud-rack whence the moon has passed away.
> Her paths without her? Day's appointed sway   5
>   Usurped by desolate night. Her pillowed place
>   Without her? Tears, ah me! for love's good grace
> And cold forgetfulness of night or day.
>
> What of the heart without her? Nay, poor heart,
>   Of thee what word remain ere speech be still?   10
>   A wayfarer by barren ways and chill,
> Steep ways and weary, without her thou art,
>   Where the long cloud, the long wood's counterpart,
>   Sheds doubled darkness up the labouring hill.

Rossetti's effects are quite different from, say, Milton's. His sound
does not swell. It is in the jostling and artful repetition of vowels
and consonants, the juxtaposition of opposed sounds and opposed
feet that the poet gains his effects. The first quatrain presents the
finest example I know in Rossetti of his "musical" virtuosity. The
poem rises very effectively to that image of the moon passing away.
When the moon is mentioned the rhythm changes (from "cloud-
rack" on).

With Rossetti we have come almost full circle in subject matter, back to the love sonnet. By now, however, the sonnet has taken
other realms of experience as its subject, has loosened its rhythms,
and has occasionally forsaken iambic pentameter. The most im-
pressive sonnets of recent times have been those, like Hopkins' or
Dowson's, which do not strike us immediately as sonnets at all, but
yet require the discipline of that demanding verse form. Yeats'
"Leda and the Swan" is a good example:

> A sudden blow: the great wings beating still
> Above the staggering girl, her thighs caressed
> By the dark webs, her nape caught in his bill,

He holds her helpless breast upon his breast.
How can those terrified vague fingers push   5
The feathered glory from her loosening thighs?
And how can body laid in that white rush,
But feel the strange heart beating where it lies?
A shudder in the loins engenders there
The broken wall, the burning roof and tower   10
And Agamemnon dead.
            Being so caught up,
So mastered by the brute blood of the air,
Did she put on his knowledge with his power
Before the indifferent beak could let her drop?

Yeats' sonnet is one of the few we have examined in which there is no speaker intimately involved with the action, speaking as it directly affects him. The love convention always called for such involvement. Here the poem raises essential questions about man's nature by examining an ancient myth in which Zeus was supposed to have come to Leda as a swan after which she gave birth to two eggs which hatched Castor and Pollux, Helen of Troy, and Clytemnestra, murderess of her husband Agamemnon. The result of this convergence of man and godhead apparently is conflict between the two aspects of man, of which man is now aware — his animal and spiritual qualities. War and murder follow. The poem raises the moment into importance by its drama, which befits the metaphysical and psychological meanings with which Yeats invested it. It tries not to solve the problem of man's nature, but instead to leave us contemplating a paradox.

In his revisions of this sonnet Yeats strove for drama. If in this case we do not feel that the poet is intimately involved in the action, we are drawn into the situation by the sudden appearance of Zeus. We see it all happen neither sooner nor later than Leda does, and she *is* involved. Here are various revisions which Yeats made of the first quatrain before he was satisfied:

(1) Now can the swooping godhead have his will
    Yet hovers, though her helpless thighs are pressed
    By the webbed toes; and that all powerful bill
    Has suddenly bowed her face upon his breast.

(2) The swooping godhead is half hovering still
Yet climbs upon her trembling body pressed
By the webbed toes, and that all powerful bill
Can hold her helpless body on his breast.

(3) A swoop upon great wings and hovering still
The bird descends, and her frail thighs are pressed

(4) A rush, a sudden wheel and hovering still
The bird descends, and her frail thighs are pressed
By the webbed toes, and that all-powerful bill
Has laid her helpless face upon his breast.

Finally:

A sudden blow: the great wings beating still
Above the staggering girl, her thighs caressed
By the dark webs, her nape caught in his bill,
He holds her helpless breast upon his breast.

It is clear in what direction Yeats was moving, and his revision demonstrates that he did not consider the sonnet form a confinement. Instead he clearly was using it to give a shape to his poem against which rhythm and sound could profitably beat for their effects. He saw his poem as an artifice.

Some Suggested Reading

John, L. C., *The Elizabethan Sonnet Sequences*.
Tomlinson, C., *The Sonnet, Its Origin, Structure, and Place in Poetry*.

4

Metaphysical Poetry:

ARGUMENT INTO DRAMA

What is "metaphysical"? Characteristics of the style. Diction, rhythm, conceit, wit: Donne's "Twicknam Garden." Marvell's "To His Coy Mistress": argument and drama. Religious verse: Herbert. Cavalier lyric: Lovelace. Influence on the moderns.

1

Verse form is only one aspect of poetic form. A sonnet, as we have seen, can be written in a variety of styles, each age and each poet within the age developing his own particular voice. Another approach to poetry is, therefore, through style. Our subject in this chapter is a particular poetic style known as "metaphysical," so named by John Dryden with reference to the poetry of John Donne (1573–1631) and by Samuel Johnson with reference generally to English poetry written during the first half of the seventeenth century. It has been looked upon as a poetry in revolt against Petrarchanism, artifice, and outworn Elizabethan techniques; but this view is too extreme. It is better seen as a development out of Elizabethan poetry, some of its qualities being present as early as Wyatt. "Metaphysical" poetry is, however, primarily associated with Donne, and many of its characteristics are simply those of that very individualistic poet, developed and exploited throughout the rest of the seventeenth century. Donne's poetry has a considerable variety, but for convenience we may note that his love lyrics (*Songs and Sonnets*, published 1633) and his later religious verse (mainly the *Holy Sonnets*) provide the two main lines of influence upon later metaphysical poets. In the tradition of religious verse are George Herbert (1593–1633), Richard Crashaw (1613?–1649), and Henry Vaughan (1622–1695). In the secular tradition are Lord Herbert of Cherbury (1583–1648), Aurelian Townshend (c.1583–c.1651), John Cleveland (1613–1658), Abraham Cowley (1618–1667), and Andrew Marvell (1621–1678). Another group of poets who took their inspiration mainly from the poet and dramatist Ben Jonson (1572–1637) were somewhat near the influence of Donne: Robert Herrick (1591–1674), Thomas Carew (1595?–1639?), Sir John Suckling (1609–1642), and Richard Lovelace (1618–1657).[1] So much for names.

Dryden's first characterization of Donne's poetry as "metaphysical" occurs in the following passage:

> He affects the metaphysics, not only in his satires but in his amorous verses where nature only should reign; and perplexes the minds of the fair sex with nice speculations of philosophy when he should engage their hearts and entertain them with the softness of love.[2]

Metaphysics is a branch of philosophy dealing with first principles, the nature of being (ontology), or the structure of the universe (cosmology). In the strict sense of the word, Donne is not metaphysical at all; Dryden may simply have meant that Donne employs imagery drawn from science. Among the great metaphysical poems (in the usual sense of the term) are Lucretius' *De Rerum Natura*, Dante's *Divine Comedy*, and Goethe's *Faust*, poems with an encyclopedic cosmological interest. Such poems are bound to be long, to be concerned with creation and apocalypse, or the extremes of imaginative desire and repugnance, heaven and hell. The sort of "metaphysical" poem with which we are concerned is rarely more than a few pages long and does not necessarily or even generally have the interests just described. "Metaphysical" has come to denote the style of which Donne's poetry is the exemplar.

---

[1] See George Williamson, *The Donne Tradition*, New York, 1958.
[2] "A Discourse concerning the Origin and Progress of Satire," *Of Dramatic Poesy and Other Essays* (George Watson, ed.), New York, 1962, II, p. 76.

Several things strike us at once about Donne's poetry: unashamed use of wide and often obscure learning, colloquial diction and rhythm, variety of stanzaic pattern, intellectual wit, use of logical argument, and analytical detachment. Each of these characteristics is worth illustrating. Donne and the metaphysicals draw imagery from all the branches of learning, from alchemy, geography, geometry, medicine, and medieval scholastic philosophy. For instance, Donne expresses his emotions by a "nice speculation" about the nature of angels:

> Twice or thrice had I loved thee,
> Before I knew thy face or name;
> So in a voice, so in a shapelesse flame,
> *Angells* affect us oft.
>
> ("Aire and Angells")

Or he can employ geography and geometry to express the total commitment of his love:

> On a round ball
> A workman that hath copies by, can lay
> An Europe, Afrique, and an Asia,
> And quickly make that, which was nothing, *All*,
> So doth each teare,
> Which thee doth weare,
> A globe, yea world by that impression grow,
> Till thy teares mixt with mine doe overflow
> This world, by waters sent from thee, my heaven
> dissolved so.
>
> ("A Valediction: Of Weeping")

This use of the mundane but unusual comparison is combined with a mundane diction, a colloquial style:

> I wonder by my troth, what thou and I
> Did, till we lov'd? Were we not wean'd till then?
> But suck'd on countrey pleasures, childishly?
>
> ("The Good-morrow")

or:

Busie old foole, unruly Sunne,
    Why dost thou thus,
Through windowes, and through curtaines call on us?
Must to thy motions lovers seasons run?
    Sawcy pedantique wretch, goe chide
    Late schoole boyes. . . .

                          ("The Sunne Rising")

Very rarely, and then only in brief passages, is Donne incantatory
or "evocative" in his rhythms. Here is a typical passage of Tennyson to set against the passages above:

Old yew, which graspest at the stones
    That name the underlying dead,
    Thy fibres net the dreamless head,
Thy roots are wrapped about the bone.

                          ("In Memoriam")

Even in his most "lyrical" mood Donne begins a poem with a line
in which the rhythm does not predict the dominant pattern, as in
the opening line below:

As virtuous men passe mildly away,
    And whisper to their soules, to goe,
Whilst some of their sad friends do say,
    The breath goes now, and some say, no.

        (From "A Valediction: Forbidding Mourning")

The first two stanzas of "Lover's Infiniteness" (below) reflect
Donne's rhythmic freedom, his lack of dependence upon sensuous
vividness in imagery, and, equally important, his use of argument
as a structural device. The argument is easily lost, and it must
therefore be closely followed. Certainly this is a poem Dryden
thought would perplex the minds of the fair sex:

If yet I have not all thy love,
Deare, I shall never have it all,
I cannot breathe one other sigh, to move,

Nor can intreat one other teare to fall,
And all my treasure, which should purchase thee, 5
Yet no more can be due to mee
Sighs, teares, and oathes, and letters I have spent,
Then at the bargaine made was ment,
If then thy gift of love were partiall,
That some to mee, some should to others fall, 10
    Deare, I shall never have Thee All.

Or if then thou gavest mee all,
All was but All, which thou hadst then,
But if in thy heart, since, there be or shall,
New love created bee, by other men, 15
Which have their stocks intire, and can in teares,
In sighs, in oathes, and letters outbide mee,
This new love may beget new feares,
For, this love was not vowed by thee.
And yet it was, thy gift being generall, 20
The ground, thy heart is mine, what ever shall
    Grow there, deare, I should have it all.

A closely reasoned argument which makes "nice speculations," the poem also uses a minimum of sensuous vividness and depends upon generalized language for its effects. The poem does not reject lyricism, but rather uses it sparingly beneath the colloquial, conversational tone.

Donne's imagery frequently, then, requires that the reader follow his thought intellectually rather than sensuously. The following lines from one of Donne's most famous poems, "The Extasie," illustrate this practice. The poet is speaking of two lovers sitting on a bank, holding hands.

As 'twixt two equal Armies, Fate
    Suspends uncertaine victorie,
Our soules, (which to advance their state,
    Were gone out,) hung 'twixt her, and mee.
And whil'st our souls negotiate there,
    We like sepulchrall statues lay.

The imagery is not visual. Its very abstractness is suggestive of a supersensuous tension. And "tension" is surely the right word here when we consider the mention of armies and uncertain victory. The language is very precise. The word "negotiate" is particularly successful with its overtones of formal discussion or accomplishment by diplomacy. The word "suspends" very effectively supports the idea of tension between the bodies. Not only do the souls represent the fates of the lovers as contending armies, but the souls are envoys of their bodies. "Sepulchrall statues" presents a visual image of a sort, but it is not vivid; the feeling it generates comes from its aura of death, immobility and quiet, and its sibilant alliteration. Because the poem as a whole refuses to divorce the body from the soul, the selves are described as remaining within the lovers' bodies. The souls as envoys suggest only a tentative and not finally satisfactory relationship. It is not surprising that T. S. Eliot should, on the basis of lines like these, have written of Donne's "sensuous apprehension of thought," [3] even though close examination shows Donne's imagery not to be particularly concrete. Perhaps it would do as well to say that Donne often expresses human situations by describing sensuous experience in terms of abstract relations.

If Donne's effects are not toward sensuous vividness, they must move in another direction: perhaps toward the rapid movement of thought — the development of an idea or a feeling through the quick association of unlikely things. Donne exhibits a habit of making fine distinctions, as in these stanzas from "A Valediction: Forbidding Mourning":

> Dull sublunary lovers love
>   (Whose soule is sense) cannot admit
> Absence, because it doth remove
>   Those things which elemented it.
>
> But we by a love, so much refin'd,
>   That our selves know not what it is,
> Inter-assured of the mind,
>   Care lesse, eyes, lips, and hands to misse.

[3] "The Metaphysical Poets," *Selected Essays*, 1917–1932, New York, 1932, p. 246.

Our two soules therefore, which are one,
    Though I must goe, endure not yet
A breach, but an expansion,
    Like gold to ayery thinnesse beat.

If they be two, they are two so
    As stiffe twin compasses are two,
Thy soule the fixt foot makes no show
    To move, but doth, if th'other doe.

And though it in the center sit,
    Yet when the other far doth rome,
It leans, and hearkens after it,
    And grows erect, as that comes home.

Such wilt thou be to me, who must
    Like th'other foot, obliquely runne;
Thy firmnes makes my circle just,
    And makes me end, where I begunne.

What Donne most obviously employs here is the conceit, a device typical of metaphysical verse. The term originally merely meant an idea, but as a poetic device it came to mean the development of a figure of speech which presents an unusual parallel between two apparently unrelated things. T. S. Eliot has described the metaphysical use of the conceit as "the elaboration . . . of a figure of speech to the farthest stage to which ingenuity can take it." [4] The metaphysical use of the conceit is "intellectual" in that it requires the reader to think out distant relationships, not merely apprehend a likeness between two things on the basis of what is available to the senses. The conceit is therefore unlikely to be what the nineteenth-century reader, for example, thought of as "poetic." It may at first glance appear far-fetched, even poetically perverse.

The first conceit above occurs in the third quoted stanza. It is a "condensed" conceit, in that Donne does not develop it at any length. Instead he passes on to another longer or "expanded" conceit. The condensed conceit presents the idea of gold being beaten out so thin as to be transparent, expanded indefinitely but remaining a single sheet. It is an intellectual figure of no primary sensu-

[4] *Ibid.*, p. 242.

ousness. It fixes the relationship of the parted lovers. The second, expanded conceit is perhaps the most famous in metaphysical poetry. Developed through three stanzas, its basic figure of the drawing-compasses presents nothing which is sensuous and directly applicable to the lovers. It is the application of abstract relationships that strikes us. The poet is not interested in the objects so much as in the relations between the objects. A geometric figure is certainly proper to such an interest, because geometry itself is concerned with relations, not with existent or tangible objects. Too "visual" a reading actually destroys the figure: In the last stanza, where the speaker ends where he began, Donne means to indicate that he returns inevitably to the beloved because of her "firmness," to which he is attached. But taken visually, we know that he merely makes a circle around the beloved. Donne certainly does not intend to indicate this circle as the exact form of the speaker's trip. (We could, I suppose, extend the figure mentally and imagine the person using the compass to close it and restore the lovers to each other.) But it is clear, I think, that Donne's image must not be taken visually but abstractly and verbally. The play is on words, not primarily on sensuous images. The image is far-fetched only if we demand at every stage strict literal interpretations. Instead the image establishes a group of relationships: sensitivity of one to the other, tension between them as one "harkens" after the other and follows it though while at the same time remaining stationary. All the relations, including erotic suggestion, present the totality of the lovers' relationship.

The conceit is a product of what we may call "wit." But wit has had many meanings — some of them are preserved in "to wit," "witness," and "half-witted." Today we usually mean by "witty" something amusing or funny. But as used to explain the source of the conceit "wit" refers to something that arises out of the intellect. Eliot has described metaphysical wit as follows:

> . . . we can say that wit is not erudition; it is sometimes stifled by erudition, as in much of Milton. It is not cynicism, though it has a kind of toughness which may be confused with cynicism by the tender-minded. It is confused with erudition because it

belongs to an educated mind; rich in generations of experience; and it is confused with cynicism because it implies a constant inspection and criticism of experience. It involves probably a recognition implicit in the expression of every experience, of other kinds of experience which are possible.[5]

Wit, then, requires and expresses a certain kind of objectivity. Its attempt is to see the object or the action whole or from various points of view simultaneously. This may involve seeing things as both good and bad, pleasant and disagreeable, serious and comical. It is an essentially rational perception of things, and the metaphysical conceit is one effective means of expressing such perception. Samuel Johnson (1709–1784), the greatest critic of his age, who was not always favorably impressed by the metaphysical poets, described wit as it appears in their work as follows:

> . . . wit . . . may be more rigorously and philosophically considered as a kind of *discordia concors*; a combination of dissimilar images, or discovery of occult resemblances in things apparently unlike. Of wit, thus defined [the metaphysical poets] have more than enough. The most heterogeneous ideas are yoked by violence together; nature and art are ransacked for illustrations, comparisons, and allusions; their learning instructs and their subtilty surprises; but the reader commonly thinks his improvement dearly bought, and, though he sometimes admires, is seldom pleased.[6]

Dr. Johnson wrote from the point of view of a later age in which the metaphysical impulse had worn itself out in uninteresting discords. Such a weakness is always possible among the metaphysicals. Donne's "The Flea" tempts absurdity, and Marvell inadvertently achieves it in these lines (even though in context their aim is not at all solemn). The cleverness is simply extended too far:

> But now the *Salmon-Fishers* moist
> Their *Leathern Boats* begin to hoist;
> And, like *Antipodes* in Shoes
> Have shod their Heads in their *Canoes.*

> ("Upon Appleton House")

[5] "Andrew Marvell," *op. cit.,* p. 262.
[6] "Abraham Cowley," *Lives of the English Poets,* available in *The Great Critics* (J. H. Smith and E. W. Parks, ed.), p. 461.

The foremost critic of a later age, Coleridge, also complained of this kind of image, thinking it fanciful rather than imaginative: "The Fancy brings together images which have no connexion natural or moral, but are yoked together by the poet by means of some accidental coincidence." He gives as an example lines from *Hudibras* by Samuel Butler (1612–1680):

> The sun had long since in the lap
> Of Thetis taken out his nap,
> And like a lobster boyl'd the morn
> From black to red began to turn.

But Coleridge's definition of imagination requires for its appearance in a work of art "the balance or reconcilement of opposite or discordant qualities." [7] And Johnson himself qualifies his derogatory remarks with the following: ". . . if they frequently threw away their wit upon false conceits, they likewise sometimes struck out unexpected truth; if their conceits were far-fetched, they were often worth the carriage. To write on their plan, it was at least necessary to read and think." [8] Conceits "worth the carriage" are greatly admired among poets and critics of our own time. I. A. Richards values ironic detachment, and describes irony as "bringing in of the opposite." [9] Cleanth Brooks in his two books, *Modern Poetry and the Tradition* and *The Well Wrought Urn*, values highly the poem in which "disparities are recognized and deliberately exploited by the poet." [10]

But before we consider this modern interest, we must look closely at a few poems which present different aspects of the metaphysical style.

[7] *Selected Poetry and Prose*, p. 275.
[8] *Op. cit.*, p. 462.
[9] *Principles of Literary Criticism*, New York, 1928, p. 250.
[10] His position is clearly stated in "The Language of Paradox," *The Well Wrought Urn*, New York, 1947, pp. 3–20.

II

It is proper to begin with, or in this case return to, Donne, a controversial poet even today. "Done [sic], for not keeping of accent, deserved hanging," said his contemporary Ben Jonson, and then qualified his statement by asserting Donne to be ". . . the first poet in the world in some things." [11] Though Donne seems from our point of view to have made the language of poetry more "natural," Carew praises him in his "Elegie" for having maintained decorous artificiality. Examination of poetic theory of the time, such as has been made by Rosemond Tuve, suggests that Donne's colloquial language is representative of an acceptable kind of renaissance style. His style is normally that of satire or dialectic, the decorum of which required the homely phrase. His normal poetic structure is the "deliberative oration," which as one of the typical structures of renaissance rhetoric had as its aim to persuade or dissuade, praise or dispraise. Miss Tuve explains:

> Although, as in rhetoric, there is more stress on moving the affections than on revealing them, poetry of this genre is expected to be especially "simple, sensuous and passionate." The note of emphasis upon an appraisal, an evaluation, and thence frequently upon undisguised persuasion, is even so the note which is never lost. This explains in part the presence of so much general statement in songs, for, instead of being personal revelations, they are praises or dispraises . . . or they plead for or against something.[12]

Metaphor was meant to delight the reader, as the conceit usually does, by a display of intellectual agility and by deepening the significance of the poem. Metaphor was not employed necessarily to make the poem more concrete or visual. The tendency was actually toward abstraction. Both Elizabethan and metaphysical poets (particularly the latter) seem to find value in logical structure in their poems. We have already seen these tendencies at work in the sonnet — Shakespeare's, for example. The Shakespearean son-

[11] *Conversations with William Drummond of Hawthorndon*, New York, 1923, pp. 4, 6.
[12] *Elizabethan and Metaphysical Imagery*, pp. 84–86.

net, with its rigid delineation of parts, is a natural vehicle for argument. But Donne, except in the *Holy Sonnets*, tended to employ the lyrical form even where the thrust of the poem was argumentative. This choice gives a lively effect to his arguments, and allows for considerable variety and more unexpected changes in pace and tone. But Donne's arguments are primarily pseudo-arguments, that is, arguments by analogy, by a rapid association of ideas which gives the effect of the speaker's discovering his own thought only as he expresses it. As an example, let us take his "Twicknam Garden":

> Blasted with sighs, and surrounded with tears,
>   Hither I come to seeke the spring,
>   And at mine eyes, and at mine eares,
> Receive such balmes, as else cure every thing;
>   But O, selfe traytor, I do bring   5
> The spider love, which transubstantiates all,
>   And can convert Manna to gall,
> And that this place may thoroughly be thought
>   True Paradise, I have the serpent brought.
>
> 'Twere wholsomer for mee, that winter did   10
>   Benight the glory of this place,
>   And that a grave frost did forbid
> These trees to laugh, and mocke mee to my face;
>   But that I may not this disgrace
> Indure, nor yet leave loving, Love let mee   15
>   Some senslesse piece of this place bee;
> Make me a mandrake, so I may groane here,
>   Or a stone fountaine weeping out my yeare.
>
> Hither with christall vyalls, lovers come,
>   And take my teares, which are loves wine,   20
>   And try your mistresse Teares at home,
> For all are false, that tast not just like mine;
>   Alas, hearts do not in eyes shine,
> Nor can you more judge womans thoughts by teares,
>   Than by her shadow, what she weares.   25
> O perverse sexe, where none is true but shee,
>   Who's therefore true, because her truth kills mee.

The poem is full of unusual language — the surprising use of
"spider," the introduction of the serpent, the adjective "grave"
with its deathly overtones. Rhythmically it is also unusual, setting
out as dactylic trimeter which promptly becomes dominantly
iambic with alternating lines of tetrameter and pentameter.[13]
Many of the lines have powerful variations; and the whole
rhythmic arrangement provides the right tension between colloquial looseness and meditative smoothness.

At first the speaker is self-consciously depressed at the refusal of
the lady (probably the Countess of Bedford) to be unfaithful to
her husband. As he proceeds, his own ingenuity weaves a web of
argument. The images which describe his state lead him to a
greater awareness of the paradoxical nature of his experience and
his surroundings. Soon he is launched forth on meditation which
ends in an argument or diatribe against the lady's cruelty. He is a
"selfe traytor" who has brought with him a "spider love." The
phrase itself is ominous, but Donne is every bit as interested in the
possible intellectual extensions of the image as in its direct sensuousness. The spider's system converts what it devours into the
web which catches things to devour — manna to gall, so to speak.
The process is cyclical and endless, dark and forbidding, a perversion of love into a cruel domination. The image seems to fire the
speaker to create an even more depressing image. This garden is
properly a place of spring, joy, new birth, innocence, and love. But,
aware of his own contrary feelings of depression, he associates himself with the only dark thing that properly inhabits such a Paradise
— the Biblical serpent of Eden. Both creatures — spider and serpent — are lowly, unpleasant, often poisonous creatures. Thus the
progression from image to image is by "logical" association.

Having introduced these foreign creatures into the garden as
representative of the state of his love affair (but not completely

---

[13] It is difficult to know just how Donne and his contemporaries read some of
his lines. Perhaps in many cases the lines seemed more regular to them than
they do today, for accents may not have been so fixed in Donne's time.

foreign, since every garden must have its serpent after all), he then develops this thought by considering the impropriety of the garden as a surrounding for himself. It should at least be winter for him to be in tune with the place. But let that be, he thinks; there must be some object he can become that will adequately symbolize his state. A mandrake is a possibility, but he chooses to develop the image of a stone fountain. It is something more dead and cold than a mandrake, and besides it weeps water — symbolic of his tears of chagrin at the lady's faithfulness.

Through the last stanza the poem plays with our sense of the meaning of "truth." Three possible meanings seem to lie in the background. The dominant one is marital faithfulness. Secondary are conformity to nature and the simple facts of a situation. The speaker, satisfied with his fountain metaphor, first asserts that his tears present a partial standard of truth, by which love can be measured. Tears of the faithful will taste like his. Alas, however, they are no final proof of faithfulness, since hearts are not tears and do not necessarily shine forth, like tears in the eyes. Therefore, one must not judge a woman's thoughts by her tears, even though faithful women will cry tears like his. It is also true (or natural) of women to be untrue (unfaithful). In this sense the sex is perverse: Their true nature is to be untrue. His lady is, however, faithful to her husband, which makes her untrue to her sex and in that sense a perversion of the natural perversity of her sex. The poem concludes by pointing out that this perverse faithfulness on her part is destroying him. We might add that all the possible truths in the situation contribute to his state: female perversity, perverse faithfulness, and the simple facts. At the end the poem turns upon a conceit involving a play with meaning.

Donne's poem is both argument and meditation. In spite of its "nice speculations" and its ambiguous language it has a kind of drama. Cleanth Brooks has made this point:

> Donne's poems are dramatic — not only fundamentally but on the most obvious level. There are the dialogues between the poet and his mistress, or between the poet and his God, or between the various selves of the poet. There are the swift, abrupt openings;

there are the sudden shifts of tone. There is the use of shock, and
the sudden turn of thought which leads to an unexpected climax.
To turn to deeper and more significant characteristics, the poet's
approach to any given subject, however abstract or general it may
be, is always made through some concrete situation.[14]

"Twicknam Garden," if it is dramatic, has affinities to the soliloquy in drama. The exceptions to the analogue are important. First,
there is no play. The poem *contains* what drama there is. Second,
the speaker seems a little more detached, a little more capable of
seeing all sides of his situation — more, even, than Hamlet in his
most objective mood.

III

Taken as dramatic, Donne's poem is a sort of soliloquy. Only one
person is present. The speaker only ideally addresses other lovers
and the whole female sex. Nevertheless, the poem at the same time
has characteristics of a sort of address. The speaker is obliquely
addressing some specific person — usually the lady. Most of
Donne's songs are of this nature, but as an example of this sort of
drama, I choose a famous poem by the later metaphysical poet,
Andrew Marvell. The poem is "To His Coy Mistress," in which
the speaker seems actually to be addressing someone. And yet the
situation is not as it is in the usual so-called dramatic monologue.
We need not, in fact should not, infer the existence and actions
of the listener from the words, as we do in, say, Browning's "My
Last Duchess." There is further a sense that the speaker is also
speaking to himself. We need not, in other words, go so far as to
place the speaker on a stage, infer the nature of the scenery, the
other characters, and so forth. Metaphysical "drama" is more abstract than that:

> Had we but World enough, and Time,
> This coyness Lady were no crime.
> We would sit down, and think which way
> To walk, and pass our long Loves Day.

[14] *Modern Poetry and the Tradition*, Chapel Hill, 1939, p. 213.

Thou by the *Indian Ganges* side   5
Should'st Rubies find: I by the Tide
Of *Humber* would complain. I would
Love you ten years before the Flood:
And you should if you please refuse
Till the Conversion of the *Jews*.   10
My vegetable Love should grow
Vaster than Empires, and more slow.
An hundred years should go to praise
Thine Eyes, and on thy Forehead Gaze.
Two hundred to adore each Breast: 15
But thirty thousand to the rest.
An Age at least to every part,
And the last Age should show your Heart.
For Lady you deserve this State;
Nor would I love at lower rate.   20
   But at my back I alwaies hear
Times winged Charriot hurrying near:
And yonder all before us lye
Desarts of vast Eternity?
Thy beauty shall no more be found;   25
Nor, in thy marble Vault, shall sound
My ecchoing Song: then Worms shall try
That long preserv'd Virginity:
And your quaint Honour turn to dust;
And into ashes all my Lust.   30
The Grave's a fine and private place,
But none I think do there embrace.
   Now therefore, while the youthful hew
Sits on thy skin like morning dew
And while thy willing Soul transpires   35
At every pore with instant Fires,
Now let us sport us while we may;
And now, like am'rous birds of prey,
Rather at once our Time devour,
Than languish in his slow-chapt pow'r   40
Let us roll all our Strength, and all
Our sweetness, up into one Ball:
And tear our Pleasures with rough strife,
Thorough the Iron gates of Life.
Thus, though we cannot make our Sun   45
Stand still, yet we will make him run.

We have observed already the metaphysical poet's tendency to reflect all sides of his experience. He is discontented with easy solutions which head or heart alone provides. The poem's resolution is seldom the victory of one direct view over another but a completed tension of opposites such as Coleridge demanded in his definition of a poem as "unity in multeity." The speaker argues to his coy mistress subtly on the "gather rosebuds" theme. Analysis will disclose that the poem wears the harness of logic but not the bit. Take the three verse paragraphs: Each begins as part of a progressive argument — "Had we . . . ," "But . . . ," "Now therefore . . . ." But the argument, though convincing in one way, is qualified by the poet's tone, by imagery which reveals another side to his feelings. As we read, our assumption that the drama is merely one of seduction is weakened. We see now that the poem is about love, time, and death, and that even to classify it in that way does not reach its center. Too much of its meaning lies in its tone, which paraphrase fails to convey. The poem should, therefore, be read as if it were spoken dramatically. What I shall say about the poem has mainly to do, then, with the tone. The reader's job is similar to an actor's in interpreting how a speech should properly be delivered.

The poem begins with a sort of controlled exasperation. The speaker is in middle dudgeon over the lady's insistence on the proprieties of their love relationship (the poem is, among other things, satirical of Petrarchan love conventions and achieves satire in one of the usual ways: by bringing things down to the "realistic" situation behind the "artificial" forms of action). The rhythm suggests a slight impertinence: the delay after "enough" in the first line, the similar delay in line 12 before the flippant line is completed, the simple word "long" (recalling, incidentally, Wyatt's "The long love . . .") seems to suggest the speaker's disdain for the kind of love affair he is describing (the same kind that Wyatt takes quite seriously). The speaker's point, of course, is that time passes, that the forms of courtship which the "romantic" situation demands devour the lovers' lives pointlessly. Lines 5 to 20 expand upon line 1. There is something terrifically egocentric, the speaker implies, about his mistress' demands for the love conventions. It is as if she really thought that she and her lover were the only people alive and that, furthermore, they would live forever. Assuming these far-fetched notions to be true, in respect to space she *could* hunt exotic rubies on the banks of the romantic Ganges while he played the pathetic lover complaining on the banks of the mundane Humber. In respect to time, he *could* devote ages to the adoration of each part of her (here he *insists* on being sensual). Time and space come together in the flippant, disdainful (yet comic for their almost disgusting giganticism) lines:

> My vegetable Love should grow
> Vaster than Empires, and more slow.

The verse paragraph ends with a line (20) which playfully suggests the extent of his virility and at the same time continues his ironic insistence on the code.

Now, however, having given one side of the case (ironically), he must prove *his* side. The images he presents are full of foreboding, even terror; but the tone is almost one of glee. The speaker gains some revenge over the lady by tormenting her with the images of graves and worms. He even reminds her, by implication (lines 31–32), of her own desire for him, while at the same time warning her that she may never fulfill that desire.

After this devastating "proof" of his side of the argument, he concludes. But even as the conclusion in which his logic will triumph begins, the image of death, which he introduced to torture *her*, rears up to torture *him*. He reveals to himself some necessary reservations about his own argument. In making love they will be birds of prey eating at the body of their own lives (worms, at least, eat only the dead). We are, I think, invited to turn back to the mistress' view and see some virtue in it after all, even as the argument locks home in the final couplet. In neither way can man win over time. Is either way worth the trouble? A note of asceticism seems to lurk beneath the dominant argument. The speaker's argument is pursued to the end but not without a sense of conflict in the lovers' relationship. Ultimately the speaker's argument is not even logically convincing. Its appeal is finally to the mistress' sense of excitement at living and loving in the face of inevitable defeat. The poem begins as argument, ends as drama.

Marvell employs images of hardness and coldness to describe love not only in "To His Coy Mistress" but also in "The Definition of Love":

> But Fate does Iron wedges drive,
> And alwaies crouds it self betwixt,

which combines with a Donnean conceit:

> And therefore her Decrees of Steel
> Us as the distant Poles have plac'd,
> (Though Loves whole World on us doth wheel)
> Not by themselves to be embrac'd.

The poem develops this conceit through its remaining three stanzas. Marvell's poetry is by and large "smoother" than Donne's, less complex in its rhythms. But it remains clearly in Donne's tradition in respect to imagery and the dramatic structure of argument.

IV

Marvell's poems are generally representative of the secular line of metaphysical poetry. The tradition as a whole contains a good amount of religious verse, from Donne's *Holy Sonnets* through some of the poetry of our own time — Eliot's, for example. George Herbert, an Anglican divine who knew Donne, is one of the major figures in this line. If the metaphysical love lyricist affected the metaphysics in his poems, the metaphysical religious poet developed drama out of traditional theological paradoxes, such as the concept of man's fortunate fall from grace. Herbert's "Easter Wings" centers upon such a paradox. Written so that on the printed page it forms wings, it effects by its compression and then expansion of line and its final alliteration a swoop, a fall, and a rise parallel to the fall and redemption which are its subject. The first stanza:

> Lord, who createdst man in wealth and store,
>> Though foolishly he lost the same,
>>> Decaying more and more,
>>>> Till he became
>>>>> Most poore:
>>>>> With thee
>>>>> O let me rise
>>>> As larks, harmoniously,
>>> And sing this day thy victories:
> Then shall the fall further the flight in me.

Herbert apparently considered himself a simple poet, but it is characteristic of the metaphysical poet that he should employ an image of some ingenuity to make even that point:

> Who sayes that fictions onely and false hair
> Become a verse? Is there in truth no beautie?
> Is all good structure in a winding stair?

("Jordan")

In his disavowals of complexity there are touches of Donne's diction and rhythm:

> Shepherds are honest people; let them sing;
> Riddle who list, for me, and pull for Prime:
> I envie no man's nightingale or spring;
> Nor let them punish me with losse of ryme,
>> Who plainly say, *My God, My King.*

("Jordan")

Herbert's complexity is usually, however, that of traditional religious analogies and emblems, of allegory which often explains its own meaning:

> Mark you the floore? that square & speckled stone,
>> Which looks so firm and strong,
>>> Is *Patience.*

("The Church-floore")

Though in isolation these lines seem not to have many dramatic possibilities, Herbert often allows his allegory to emerge from the speaker's meditation, as if it were the product of a moment's feeling:

> A broken Altar, Lord, Thy servant reares,
> Made of a heart, and cemented with teares;
>   Whose parts are as Thy hand did frame;
>   No workman's tool hath touched the same.

("The Altar")

The tradition of metaphysical religious verse merges with the symbolist tradition (to be discussed in Chapter 8) in our own time. T. S. Eliot's "Ash Wednesday" borrows a metaphysical image developed by the seventeenth-century preacher Lancelot Andrewes, who wrote:

> Now at this time is the turning of the year. . . . Every thing now turning that we also would make it *our* time to turn to God. . . . Upon this turning *cardo virtitus,* the hinge turns, of our will or evil doing forever. . . . Repentance itself is nothing but a kind of circling which circle consists of two turnings. . . . First, a turn wherein we look forward to God and with our whole heart resolve to turn to him. Then a turn again wherein we look backward to our sins wherein we have turned from God.

Eliot centers his poem, which begins "Because I do not hope to turn again . . . ," upon Andrewes' major figure, elaborating it even further in his own way.

V

Along the edge of the metaphysical tradition is a poetry closely associated with pure "song." It does not argue as intricately, relies less on esoteric learning, and holds itself back from conceits like Donne's compass image or Marvell's iron wedges. The poets of the group are not major poets, but each has contributed a handful of immensely graceful lyrics. These include Herrick's "Corinna's Going A-Maying," Suckling's "Out Upon It! I Have Loved," which suggests the informal language of Donne, and Lovelace's "Althea" poems. Lovelace's "La Bella Bona Roba," which employs the courtly imagery of hunting, in most respects strikes a tone of cavalier nonchalance typical of the school. It shows also a concern with disparate images like that of Donne:

I cannot tell who loves the Skeleton
Of a poor Marmoset, nought but boan, boan.
Give me a nakednesse with her cloath's on.

Such whose white-sattin upper coat of skin,
Cuts upon Velvet rich Incarnadin,
Ha's yet a Body (and of Flesh) within.

Sure it is meant good Husbandry in men,
Who do incorporate with Aëry leane,
T'repair their sides, and get their Ribb agen.

Hard hap unto the Huntsman that Decrees
Fat joys for all his swet, when as he sees,
After his 'Say, nought but his Keeper's Fees.

Then Love I beg, when next thou tak'st thy Bow,
Thy angry shafts, and dost Heart-chasing go,
Passe *Rascall Deare*, strike me the largest Doe.

The poem is consciously archaic in diction and subject, but it
shows metaphysical traits: the imagery of the second stanza, the
audacious application of the Adam's rib tale, the "heart–hart" pun
upon which much of the poem turns, the quick movement from
one image to another. Usually the deeper ironies of Donne and
Marvell are absent among these so-called Cavalier poets. Nevertheless, to sing as they did, it was necessary to think.

VI

The following lines, composed in the nineteen-thirties, probably
would not have been written had it not been for Donne:

Law makes long spokes of the short stakes of men,
Your well fenced out real estate of mind
No high flat of the nomad citizen
Looks over, or train leaves behind.

The imagery of spokes and wheels, the pun on "stakes," the spatial-
izing of the mental life, all suggest a relation to the metaphysicals.
The stanza is from William Empson's "Legal Fiction." Nor is the

influence limited to Empson's poetry. It pervades his very influential critical book *Seven Types of Ambiguity*, in which compression
and complexity of statement are raised to principles of poetry.
Empson's examples are taken from a variety of poets, but the most
telling of them come from the period from Shakespeare to Marvell,
where the qualities he values are most clearly available. Empson
dislikes poetry without some intellectual fibre. His methods of
verbal analysis are directed toward revealing this quality. He feels
that his methods do not limit themselves to vague statements about
atmosphere. His most famous analysis is that of the line from
Shakespeare's famous Sonnet LXXIII:

> Bare ruined choirs, where late the sweet birds sang

> . . . the comparison holds for many reasons; because ruined mon-
> astery choirs are places in which to sing, because they involve
> sitting in a row, because they are made of wood, are carved into
> knots and so forth, because they used to be surrounded by a
> sheltering building crystallised out of the likeness of a forest, and
> coloured with stained glass and painting like flowers and leaves,
> because they are now abandoned by all but the grey walls col-
> oured like the skies of winter, because the cold and Narcissistic
> charm suggested by choir-boys suits well with Shakespeare's feel-
> ing for the object of the Sonnets, and for various sociological and
> historical reasons (the protestant destruction of the monasteries;
> fear of puritanism), which it would be hard now to trace out in
> their proportions; these reasons, and many more relating the simile
> to its place in the Sonnet, must all combine to give the line its
> beauty, and there is a sort of ambiguity in not knowing which of
> them to hold most clearly in mind. Clearly this is involved in all
> such richness and heightening of effect, and the machinations of
> ambiguity are among the very roots of poetry.[15]

We can imagine this sort of thing being done with Empson's own
poems.

Often influential books of modern criticism have been greatly
influenced by metaphysical practice. I. A. Richards, in his *Principles of Literary Criticism* and *Practical Criticism*, finds Donnean

[15] *Seven Types of Ambiguity*, New York, 1947, pp. 2–3.

irony a defense against sentimentalism. Cleanth Brooks argues, in his *Modern Poetry and the Tradition*, for a tradition of poetry that rejects eighteenth century and romantic verse and appropriates the qualities of metaphysical and symbolist poetry. In a later book, *The Well Wrought Urn*, he retreats somewhat from this stand, emphasizing the paradoxical nature of poetic statement even in some eighteenth-century and romantic verse, and advising that we view poems as "dramas." But modern critics and poets have perhaps read into the work of the metaphysical poets a bit too much of their own situations. Eliot speaks of the metaphysicals' "direct sensuous apprehension of thought" or a recreation of thought into feeling: ". . . Tennyson and Browning are poets, and they think, but they do not feel their thought as immediately as the odour of a rose. A thought to Donne was an experience; it modified his sensibility." [16] The moderns, as Rosemond Tuve has suggested, exalt skill in psychological realism into the primary aim of poetry. Eliot's famous opening lines of "Prufrock" illustrate:

> Let us go then, you and I,
> When the evening is spread out against the sky
> Like a patient etherized upon a table.

The image is expressed in language typical of Donne. There are no restrictions to the "poetic." But the image itself aims more at the delineation of a pure psychological state in the speaker than is characteristic of Donne. Metaphysical images are more abstract, therefore more interpretable than this one. The metaphysicals wrote, after all, before Freud and Jung, even before Coleridge's pronouncements. They were interested in psychological states, as all poets have been, but that was not their overwhelming interest. They sought less the private world than the generalized vision more dependent upon argument and logical structure. Yet we constantly see modern poets like Auden remaking the tradition to which the metaphysicals belong in lines clearly his own but at the same time recalling the colloquialism and daring imagery of three hundred years ago:

[16] "The Metaphysical Poets," *op. cit.*, p. 247.

Simultaneously, as soundlessly,
    Spontaneously, suddenly
As, at the vaunt of the dawn, the kind
    Gates of the body fly open
To its world beyond, the gates of the mind,   5
    The horn gate and the ivory gate
Swing to, swing shut, instantaneously
    Quell the nocturnal rummage
Of its rebellious fronde, ill-favored
    Ill-natured and second-rate,   10
Disenfranchised, widowed and orphaned
    By a historical mistake:
Recalled from the shades to be a seeing being,
    From absence to be on display,
Without a name or history I wake   15
    Between my body and the day.

                                                ("Prime")

One suspects that the psychological matters Auden talks about,
Donne would have talked about today. But Donne's technique
differs from that of many moderns who are influenced by him. For
the moderns are also followers of the symbolist movement, which is
our subject in Chapter 8.

Some Suggested Reading

Brooks, Cleanth, *Modern Poetry and the Tradition.*

Eliot, T. S., *Selected Essays.*

Empson, William, *Seven Types of Ambiguity.*

Grierson, H. J. C., *Metaphysical Lyrics and Poems of the Seventeenth Century.*

Johnson, Samuel, "Cowley" from *Lives of the Poets.*

Tuve, Rosemond, *Elizabethan and Metaphysical Imagery.*

Williamson, George, *The Donne Tradition.*

5 *Essay, Epistle, and Satire:*

THE OUTER EDGE OF POETRY

> The *"truth"* that poetry expresses. Didactic and discursive tend-
> encies: the poem as a communication rather than an object for
> contemplation. Documentary naturalism. Science and psychology:
> Lucretius, Dryden. The standard of prose clarity. Verse essay: Pope
> and the epigrammatic couplet, Shapiro, Satire: Stauffer's "The
> Lemmings," Dryden, Pope. Romanticism's world: Byron. Epistle,
> occasional poem. Poetry at the outer edge still an object for con-
> templation.

1

In reading poems which seem dramatic (as we have used the
term) or plays written in a previous age we are not particularly
tempted to analyze their veracity or be concerned with the doctrine
they put forth. "To His Coy Mistress" does not lead us directly to
judgments upon its moral position. The courtly attitudes of Wyatt
do not require that we judge them proper or improper. Donne's
use of alchemy does not require that we believe it possible to find
the philosopher's stone.

Our attitude toward contemporary poets, who still have the vote,
so to speak, is curiously different. We often go straight to their
ideas: Yeats' praise of aristocracy, Pound's anti-Semitism, Eliot's
monarchism, the communism of the Auden group of the 'thirties.
We agree with, reject, or sometimes forgive these poets their be-
liefs as they appear in their poetry:

100

> Time that with this strange excuse
> Pardoned Kipling and his views,
> And will pardon Paul Claudel,
> Pardons him for writing well.
>
> (Auden, "In Memory of W. B. Yeats")

On the other hand, a poet of two or three hundred years ago is a period piece. We say we must understand his position simply as an aspect of his time. That Crashaw was Catholic becomes less important than that he was metaphysical; that medieval poets had some very queer notions about the physical universe does not make them less worthy of our attention, but in some respects even more worthy. One critic has said that the important thing about such poets is that they still tell us how it was to live under certain conditions and in the midst of certain ideas.

We have already noticed that among sonneteers the poet's impulse is not so much to say something to or about his mistress as it is to create an artifice. Literature is distinguished in this respect from both philosophy and history. Both the philosopher and historian must be judged ultimately by their ideas, the philosopher on the logical symmetry of his notions and their applicability to the varieties of our experience, and the historian on the credibility of his constructions of facts and surmises into a total view of time and human action. But the poet is judged ultimately not merely on the logical integrity of his poem or on the accuracy of its representation of real events. Instead he is judged in terms of the structural principles of poetry itself.

Nevertheless, there is a very large amount of poetry which displays a considerable doctrinal interest and a large amount concerned with the direct, careful representation of the exterior world. The writers of such poems clearly want to convince us of a particular idea or want to show us what some object or action "really" was like. If we examine the whole range of possibility in literary art we see, as Northrop Frye has pointed out, that it exists as a scale between two poles, the inward (or self-contained) and the outward. At one pole is the kind of literature that is most nearly an object for contemplation. It does not speak, but must be observed, like nature itself. An extreme example of this sort of poetry is the "symbolist" poem of nineteenth-century France, particularly that of Stéphane Mallarmé. In it the degree of reference to the outer world is diminished about as much as possible. Poetry here verges upon the obvious self-containment of music, though music too has its "outer" pole, as in certain program music and, for example, the representation of Til Eulenspiegel's falling head in Richard Strauss's opera. In a self-contained state language is observed moving in the direction of mathematics, the symbols of which are completely liberated from denoting objects. The symbolist poem represents, then, the inner edge of poetry, and as such it will be the subject of Chapter 8.

The tendency working against, but never wholly triumphing over, self-containment is best exemplified by poetry that seriously presents philosophical systems and scientific ideas as the poem's end, narrative based upon fact, many historical dramas, clearly autobiographical poems, occasional addresses to physical objects, poems that attempt to speak "the real language of men" (as in Wordsworth), all efforts toward detailed realistic description, and allegory which points systematically to historical events or displays allegiance to particular moral systems. It is clear that all poems work in at least one of these directions and usually in more than one. The extreme example of the tendency takes us outside literature altogether in the direction of scientific analysis. Within literature, at its outer edge, is not poetry but a form of prose fiction which documents its actions from real life — the naturalism of Émile Zola or of Theodore Dreiser. This fiction seeks in its various ways to eschew artifice. It bases its story upon actual happenings or makes the invented happenings absolutely believable. It invites a judgment as to its ability to describe "real life" accurately.

The subject of this chapter is poetry that exhibits tendencies to approach the outer edge. It must always be remembered that poetry's outer edge is contained well within the circle of literature in general and that no literature is purely descriptive and representational of an outer world. Even poetry that goes to the extreme of documentation is artifice, if worthy of its name.

11

The English age which produced some of the greatest poetry oriented to the outer world was that beginning with John Dryden (1631–1700) and ending sometime after the death of Alexander Pope (1688–1744). In this period, particularly as a result of the work of Newton, there were tremendous developments in the physical sciences. Scientific method naturally came to seem the one way to obtain knowledge. Poets were, of course, affected by these developments. Poetry followed suit, became more social and "objective." Much of it, like Pope's "Essay on Man," sought to present reality in the light of the most modern rationalistic thought. It is not really surprising that the formal source of inspiration for these poets was classic Roman literature.

The title Pope gave to his poem is itself instructive: "Essay on Man." The word "essay" suggests a poem existing near the outer edge of poetry. Its tradition stretches back into classical literature. Lucretius' "De Rerum Natura" is also an essay. Its subject is what today we might call science and philosophy. After the usual address to a divinity, in this case Venus, Lucretius takes up a series of subjects: the eternality of substance, the void, atoms, failures of other philosophers, infinity, etc. Like Lucretius' essay, Pope's raises fundamental issues, but his emphasis is upon man's place in the scheme of things:

> Say first, of God above, or man below,
> What can we reason, but from what we know?
> Of man, what see we but his station here,
> From which to reason, or to which refer?

Although Pope's poem is clearly an "essay," we notice even in these few lines that it is extremely mannered. In Pope's time the verse essay was invariably written in heroic couplets, a tight metrical arrangement of iambic pentameter. An occasional triplet was introduced, particularly by Dryden; but generally the poet operated within a rigid frame. It is as if the extreme outward interest in re-

spect to subject had to be balanced by a strict self-containment in
verse form.

Actually the first major practitioner of the verse essay in this
form was Dryden. His "Religio Laici," or "A Layman's Faith" is
characteristic of his subtle heroic couplet verse. The poem begins:

> Dim, as the borrow'd beams of Moon and Stars
> To *lonely, weary, wandring* Travellers
> Is *Reason* to the *Soul:* And as on high
> Those rowling Fires *discover* but the Sky
> Not light us *here;* So *Reason's* glimmering Ray
> Was lent, not to *assure* our *doubtfull* way,
> But guide us upward to a *better Day.*
> And as those nightly Tapers disappear
> When Day's bright Lord ascends our Hemisphere;
> So pale grows *Reason* at *Religions* sight;
> So *dyes* and so *dissolves* in *Supernatural Light.*
> Some few, whose Lamp shone brighter, have been led
> From Cause to Cause to *Natures* secret head;
> And found that *one first principle* must be;
> But *what,* or *who,* that UNIVERSAL He. . . .

The poem proceeds to discuss various philosophical positions:
Deism, revelation, tradition. Dryden anticipates objections to his
own views and systematically answers them. He concludes as follows:

> What then remains, but, waving each Extreme,
> The Tides of Ignorance, and Pride to stem?
> Neither so rich a Treasure to forgo;
> Nor proudly seek beyond our pow'r to know:
> Faith is not built on disquisitions vain;
> The things we *must* believe, are *few* and *plain:*
> But since men *will* believe more than they *need;*
> And every man will make *himself* a Creed,
> In doubtfull questions 'tis the safest way
> To learn what unsuspected Ancients say:
> For 'tis not likely *we* should higher Soar
> In search of Heav'n than *all the Church before:*

And finally:

> Thus Have I made my own Opinions clear:
> Yet neither Praise expect, not Censure fear:

> And this unpolish'd, rugged Verse I chose;
> As fittest for Discourse, and nearest prose.

Several typical attitudes are apparent here. The poet seeks an abstract clarity, befitting his subject. He holds that his poem is *discoursing* on something. He values tradition and thoughtful examination of evidence. Though the poem is discursive, the poet does not hesitate to employ figures of speech. These figures are clearly comparisons or simple similes illustrative of the subject. Nor are they unusual similes; indeed they are very conventional — images of ascent, light and darkness. They are useful for their unobtrusiveness and their susceptibility to extension. They have nothing of the brilliance of modern poetic imagery, which aims not at the illustration of an idea but at the direct expression of an experience. The poem's total form is fixed partially by the recurrence of these conventional figures, like motifs in music. As Dryden develops the clear, abstract, illustrative figure he makes his poem an artifice as well as a communication.

Pope, who followed Dryden with more verse essays in heroic couplets, had the greater power to invent epigrams. Many of his couplets have become almost a part of everyday language:

> A little learning is a dangerous thing;
> Drink deep, or taste not the Pierian spring.

> First follow Nature, and your judgment frame
> By her just standard, which is still the same.

> Avoid extremes; and shun the fault of such,
> Who still are pleased too little or too much.

And single lines like this one:

> For fools rush in where angels fear to tread.

All of these lines are from Pope's "Essay on Criticism," a poem which does for criticism what Boileau's "L'Art Poetique" (1674) endeavors to do for poetry: tells how it should be written. The tradition reaches back at least as far as Horace and forward to Karl Shapiro's "Essay on Rime" (1945). Pope's epigrammatic

brightness has made it difficult to see his whole poem as a formal
structure. Like most statements in poems, Pope's epigrams gain
their meaning from their context. His most famous one, for example,

> True wit is Nature to advantage dress'd;
> What oft was thought, but ne'er so well express'd,

must be understood in the light of meanings for "nature" and
"wit" implicit in the poem, particularly in relation to the examples that precede and illustrate the couplet. Pope has been speaking rather pointedly about some of the tendencies of metaphysical
verse:

> Some to Conceit alone their taste confine,
> And glittering thoughts struck out at every line;
> Pleased with a work where nothing's just or fit;
> One glaring chaos and wild heap of wit.
> Poets, like painters, thus unskill'd to trace
> The naked Nature and the living grace,
> With gold and jewels cover every part,
> And hide with ornaments their want of art.
> True wit is Nature to advantage dress'd;
> What oft was thought, but ne'er so well express'd;
> Something, whose truth convinced at sight we find,
> That gives us back the image of our mind.
> As shades more sweetly recommend the light,
> So modest plainness sets off sprightly wit.
> For works may have more wit than does 'em good,
> As bodies perish through excess of blood.

In one sense the argument here applies to more things than art,
in another it applies to nothing outside itself. The poem is sometimes anthologized in books of critical essays, but it is essentially
a poem, and we should read it not for its *own* extractable glittering
thoughts but as a verbal world in itself, operating according to its
own form. We need not reject the poem out of hand if we disagree
with some of the statements it contains.

The passage above illustrates Pope's manner fairly well. He is
not interested in the concrete sensuous image but in the gen-

eralized one. This does not prevent him from achieving vividness, for he builds up patterns of generalized imagery with considerable effect. Metaphysical verse is characterized above as "glittering" and "glaring" in a "chaos" and a "heap." He is attacking excess of decoration. The image is that of a wild heap of glittering jewels which cover up the reality of the true object. Submerged beneath this image is that of a woman laden down with jewels, which Pope brings to the forefront in his description of how wit should properly be worn. Then he proceeds with remarks about degrees of light, shade, and contrast, arguing implicitly for temperance. Then he concludes with an image of bloated grossness: the poet should not gorge himself with false wit. The imagery is there to support the statement and assist in establishing the tone.

III

Among contemporary poets Karl Shapiro has attempted a similar kind of work. Technically, however, his "Essay on Rime" is quite different. He makes no attempt to strike out the epigrammatic couplet. Writing loose decasyllabic verse, he makes the sentence and then the paragraph his main units. He eschews end-rime for the most part, though the rimes occasionally do form couplets. Generally, however, his rime is internal, and the whole poem gives the illusion of casualness. In fact, the word may be "prosiness":

> The metric of this book is made upon
> The classic English decasyllable
> Adapted to the cadence of prose speech;
> Ten units to the verse by count of eye
> Is the ground rhythm, over which is set
> The rough flux and reflux of conversation.

Shapiro's conception of imagery is quite different from Pope's and reflects the recent concern (see Chapter 8) with "suggestion" rather than illustration. This is true even though his poem is an essay in which figures of speech are essentially explanatory:

> My aim is to suggest, not to pronounce
> Sentence, or trounce the brothers of my trade;

> My wish is but to call a rose a rose
> And not a trope. . . .

In keeping with this assertion, he makes figures that have a broader range of possible significance, a "suggestivity" that we dare not pin down:

> In the mid-century of our art we leave
> The park behind and rest beside the zoo
> Of rarities. . . .

When Shapiro approaches the epigram, this more oblique use of language recalls, rather than Pope's tight constructions, Blake's enigmatic imagistic "Proverbs of Hell." I refer to the last sentence below:

> . . . To science belongs
> The isolation of knowledge, to art belongs
> The isolation of beauty; nor is it likely
> That even in this aviary can we mate two
> Creatures of such opposite feather. The owl
> Has many thoughts, the woodlark only songs.

But this wider suggestivity is sporadic, and Shapiro's danger is excessive abstraction and dullness of language and rhythm, as in the following:

> . . . Constraint was not the principle,
> And long before their manifesto laid
> The law down, certain purely transitional
> Phases set up as separate guilds, at least
> Several of which had serious influence
> And prestige which has not as yet decreased.

It is out of such passages of self-conscious prosiness that his imagery bursts suddenly:

> It argues poorly for the lesser lights
> That all their brilliance could not concentrate
> In one full ray, or do no more than splash
> The broken lengths of color into our faces.

Shapiro's verse essay, then, reflects certain changes in poetic taste. First, it moves toward the language of prose. In this respect it pushes "outwardness" even further than did the verse essayists of two hundred years ago:

> For much of modern rime denotes this bent
> To cancel out the distance and the line
> Between the language of spontaneous nature
> And that of formal artifice. . . .

On the other hand in his imagery Shapiro has not remained aloof to an opposite tendency toward "suggestion" and inwardness, set in motion primarily by the symbolist tradition. That tendency, subject here of Chapter 8, sees the image not as in itself essentially descriptive of the outer world but as part of a total form, purged of as much denotation as possible.

IV

The subject of the verse essay is usually abstract and philosophical, and the poem can adopt a variety of tone from seriously meditative to whimsical. Pope and Dryden were both masters of satire in a verse form identical to that of their serious essays. Among recent poems Donald Stauffer's "The Lemmings" stands between the serious didactic verse essay and the satire. His poem is both serious and comical as it gently jokes at its own nature. The poem is apparently about lemmings, small rodents which periodically migrate to the sea to drown themselves en masse; through his recounting of their absurd act the poet raises fundamental questions. A good many literary tastes are made fun of. The poem begins:

> Let readers say (description or abuse),
> "Pure were his morals, though his verse was loose,"

and Stauffer proceeds to describe the sources of his poetic style in a number of poets. The subject of his poem, he announces, is "lemmings, the pity of lemmings."

> A reflective poem must demonstrate wide reading.
> In such verse, too, the poet is at a loss if he

> Doesn't remind the reader he knows philosophy.
> Provided only they see that this poem is deep,
> I don't care how many people it puts to sleep.
> The special subject is lemmings. . . .

The poem proper begins with a great descriptive flourish, the seriousness of which is really mockery of the possible pompousness of such beginnings. The poet keeps falling away from his professed subject into asides about how his poem is getting along, what the reader should look for and appreciate, etc. We become aware that the poem is really an oblique "Essay on Rime." Here is an example of what I mean from the beginning of the poem:

> At a sharp, mysterious call, as though in a dream,
> The lemmings move, and down to the ocean they stream.
> From the Urals, and the Carpathians, and the plains
> Of Prussia, or Lapland, on they come in trains.
> Or secretly, through the silent forests, the hordes
> Rush to the sea in the tallest of Norway's fjords.
> For them, the whole world beckons and is on fire,
> So add what geographical names you desire:
> To say the Ganges, Peru, the Cape of Good Hope,
> Though it blur our accuracy increases our scope.
> And here I shall use T. S. Eliot's famed device
> Of allusion to gain intensity — it's nice!
> Read over Browning's *Piper of Hamelin*, please,
> Read it slowly, with care, and at your ease,
> And wherever he talks about either rats or mice
> Just substitute lemmings. Isn't *that* a device?

The philosophical problem proposed is why the lemmings drown themselves:

> If the lemmings unite to swim out to sea and die,
> The inevitable and perplexing question is *Why?*
> We might as well face it squarely and on the spot
> Without a flippant or cynical asking *Why not?*

Several reasons are advanced, including the propositions that lemmings are conscious Malthusians, that they are simply stupid, that they are feckless, reckless, etc. The poem closes with the advice that perhaps we must simply accept their act without trying to explain something we don't understand. Stauffer remarks that his conclusion "amounts almost to accepting God" rather than man as our savior, and he concludes that such an attitude will probably seem a bit odd in our age. Finally, he believes that his poem should not be attacked because it offers no answer to the problem posed:

> Give us a bit less pride and a little more trust:
> We but guess we are terribly clever; we know we are dust.
> Grace is a ware which should be on the front of our shelves,
> And we have most grace, when we don't try to make it ourselves.
> After all, reflective verse shouldn't give the answers.
> It should merely set the questions moving like dancers,
> And should leave us, where we began, with the excellent notion
> Of the lemmings moving in unison toward the ocean.

Despite its affinities to the eighteenth-century verse essay, Stauffer's poem is more oblique than its predecessors. Its ostensible subject is not its main subject. In fact, it is difficult to locate its subject precisely. In this it seems to be asserting its contemporaneity with symbolist poetry even as it invites comparison to poetry of another age. The poet seems to think of his work more as an object to be contemplated than a discursive piece. The poem's totality is the dancing movement of its own thought within the boundaries of its own form.

V

With such a poem, too, any distinction we might think necessarily exists between verse essay and satire is nearly obliterated. Satire, of course, is usually full of considerable exterior reference, even though the poet may be hiding the references by allegory, as in Dryden's "Absalom and Achitophel":

> The *Jews*, a Headstrong, Moody, Murm'ring race
> As ever tri'd th' extent and stretch of grace;

> God's pamper'd People, whom, debauch'd with ease,
> No King could govern nor no God could please. . . .

Ostensibly the subject is the Jews, but Dryden's contemporaries were invited to assume that he was really speaking about the English. Likewise they were to read Absalom as the Duke of Monmouth, Achitophel as Lord Shaftesbury:

> Of these the false *Achitophel* was first,
> A name to all succeeding Ages curst.
> For close Designs and Crooked Counsels fit,
> Sagacious, Bold, and Turbulent of wit,
> Restless, unfixt in Principles and Place,
> In Pow'r unpleased, impatient of Disgrace;
> A fiery Soul, which working out its way,
> Fretted the Pigmy Body to decay:
> And, o'r informed the Tenement of Clay.
> A daring Pilot in extremity;
> Pleas'd with the Danger, when the Waves went high
> He sought the Storms; but, for a Calm unfit,
> Would Steer too nigh the Sands to boast his Wit.
> Great Wits are sure to Madness near alli'd
> And thin Partitions do their Bounds divide.

There is something about the couplet as it is polished by poets like Dryden and Pope which invites its use in satire. In the verse essay it seems a convenient vehicle for epigrammatic pithiness, and satire preserves that quality even in a narrative framework. Dryden's attacks in "Mac Flecknoe" upon the unfortunate poet Thomas Shadwell (1642–1692) culminate periodically throughout the poem in couplets which summarize his ridiculousness, as when the prince of nonsense chooses a successor:

> This aged Prince now flourishing in Peace,
> And blest with issue of a large increase,
> Worn out with business, did at length debate
> To settle the Succession of the State;
> And pond'ring which of all his Sons was fit
> To Reign, and Wage immortal War with Wit,
> Cry'd, 'tis resolved; for Nature pleads that He

> Should onely rule, who most resembles me:
> Sh------ alone my perfect image bears,
> Mature in dullness from his tender years;
> Sh------ alone of all my Sons is he
> Who stands confirm'd in full stupidity.
> The rest to some faint meaning make pretence,
> But Sh------ never deviates into sense.
> Some Beams of Wit on other souls may fall,
> Strike through and make a lucid intervall;
> But Sh------'s genuine night admits no ray
> His rising Fogs prevail upon the Day.

One might notice how that word "deviates" ruffles the rhythm and suggests a kind of tortuousness exemplary of the distance between Shadwell and sense; or the fine invective of "genuine"; the scornful deadness of "fogs." At this point we notice also that today it means less that we know who Shadwell was than that we catch the rightness of Dryden's diction. It means less, also, that this rightness is not so much, for us, judged by its fidelity to the facts about Shadwell as it is by fidelity to the poem as a whole. If the poem has an integrity of its own the victim of satire is very quickly universalized into a type of human absurdity. Very intimate and topical satire like that of Pope in "The Dunciad" can therefore be read in later ages even if we have lost interest in the actual persons being attacked. We do not read "The Dunciad" *exactly* as Pope's contemporaries read it. But if the poet has been poetically successful we grasp no less of its beauty (as Coleridge defined the term) than his friends did. This means that the beauty of the poem does not lie ultimately in its fidelity to an external reality. Here is the beginning of Book II of that poem:

> High on a gorgeous seat, that far outshone
> Henley's gilt tub, or Fleckno's Irish throne,
> Or that where on her Curls the public pours,
> All-bounteous, fragrant grains and golden showers,
> Great Cibber sate. The proud Parnassian sneer,
> The conscious simper, and the jealous leer,
> Mix in his look: all eyes direct their rays
> On him, and crowds turn coxcombs as they gaze?

His peers shine round him with reflected grace:
New edge their dulness, and new bronze their face
So from the sun's broad beam in shallow urns
Heav'n's twinkling sparks draw light, and point their horns.

Some of its beauty does depend, however, on our knowing something of the literary universe. The passage begins as a parody of Milton's famous lines describing Satan in *Paradise Lost*. The heroic conventions are so puffed up by hyperbole that they turn inside out and convey the ridiculous. Pope's target is Colley Cibber (1671–1757), the poet laureate. In the passage mention of Cibber's name is delayed until nearly the end of the first sentence. It then appears with a pompous sibilant thud: "Great Cibber sate." He is reduced through an absurd convergence of heroic manner and mundane imagery. As twentieth-century readers we are more concerned with these suggestive overtones than with biographical information about Cibber himself. Pope has drawn Cibber into the world of his poem, into relation with other literary figures. Pope has assimilated his own experience to the conventions of literature.

VI

The major satirist of the romantic period was George Gordon, Lord Byron (1788–1824). Except for him the most important romantic poets are rather consistently serious, even solemn. Of them all, Byron is the nearest to his neoclassical predecessors. He makes some extremely unflattering remarks about "the simple Wordsworth" and the unintelligible Coleridge. His favorite poet was apparently Pope, and his language seems consciously modelled upon eighteenth-century norms. His first considerable effort at satire, "English Bards and Scotch Reviewers" (1809), is written in heroic couplets under Pope's influence. He does not excel in precise description but in generalized statement with illustrative imagery and verbal play.

As a satire, Byron's greatest poem, *Don Juan* (1818–1824), is extremely complex; for though it makes fun of Wordsworth, Coleridge, and Southey, and defends Pope, it also strikes out against some of Horace's classical strictures on how to write an epic poem:

> Most epic poets plunge 'in medias res'
>   (Horace makes this the heroic turnpike road),
> And then your hero tells, whene'er you please,
> What went before — by way of episode,
> While seated after dinner at his ease,
>   Beside his mistress in some soft abode,
> Palace, or garden, paradise, or cavern,
> Which serves the happy couple for a tavern.
>
> That is the usual method, but not mine —
>   My way is to begin with the beginning.

His choice of hero is also hardly neoclassical:

> . . . I condemn none,
>   But can't find any in the present age
> Fit for my poem (that is, for my new one);
> So, as I said, I'll take my friend Don Juan. . . .

That is, he rejects the "heroic" hero of the classical epic and insists on a contemporary one, then undercuts his insistence by allowing that contemporary life can't provide such a hero. The satire, in other words, cuts both ways.

Despite its attacks on his contemporaries, Byron's poem is characteristically romantic in that it is expressive — it holds the mirror up to Byron rather than to nature. Although Don Juan is the hero of the story line, the poem's digressions from the story are at least as important as the story itself. In the digressions Byron, himself, the poet writing the poem, is the main character, acting as if he were the deity in the poem's universe, even a manipulator of puppets. Almost anything in the narrative is capable of releasing a flow of self-expression. Describing the seashore upon which Don Juan is shipwrecked leads the narrator to thoughts of champagne and drinking in general, which occupy four stanzas, concluding as follows:

> For not the blest sherbet, sublimed with snow,
> Nor the first sparkle of the desert spring,
>   Nor Burgundy in all its sunset glow,
> After long travel, ennui, love, or slaughter,
> Vie with that draught of hock and soda-water.
>
> The coast — I think it was the coast that I
>   Was just describing — Yes, it *was* the coast —
> Lay at this period quiet as the sky. . . .

Even then he is unable to return to the story for four more stanzas.

The poem, then, gradually builds up our picture of its narrator, and the story is being used toward that end. The poem's structure might well be described as the result of a prolific struggle between a narrative objective principle and a static revelatory one.

The long poem seems to need some narrative thread even though the narrative is submerged in the personality of its author. The struggle against narrative seems typical of romantic self-expression: in Blake's *Jerusalem*, where the narrative, if there is one, is submerged in symbolic patterns; in Wordsworth's *Prelude*, where the narrative is the whole life of the author, being observed as spots of time in the memory; in Keats' *Hyperion*, which works up to the crucial action and then simply breaks off unfinished, illustrating not a struggle against narrative but perhaps a failure to achieve it.

The expression of the inner self, so characteristic of the romantics, should not be confused necessarily with the inner edge of poetry — aesthetic self-containment. If sometimes Byron seems more interested in looking into himself than outward to society, his interest is still poetically outward. Both Byron and society are a part of nature. For the romantic poet the most interesting thing in nature is the human mind; Byron reaches outward to describe *its* interior.

With all its outward interest, *Don Juan* is, of course, an object in itself. Its wit lies in the brilliance with which it manipulates the two heroes and in its sheer verbal ingenuity. Indeed, much of its humor arises from the subtle development of certain techniques. One is the almost perfect adaptation of the humorous twist to the stanzaic pattern. Don Juan, aged sixteen and inexperienced in love, becomes enamored of the young but married Donna Julia:

> Young Juan wander'd by the glassy brooks,
>   Thinking unutterable things; he threw
> Himself at length within the leafy nooks
>   Where the wild branch of the cork forest grew;
> There poets find materials for their books,
>   And every now and then we read them through,
> So that their plan and prosody are eligible,
> Unless, like Wordsworth, they prove unintelligible.
>
> He, Juan (and not Wordsworth), so pursued
>   His self-communion with his own high soul,
> Until his mighty heart, in its great mood,
>   Had mitigated part, though not the whole
> Of its disease; he did the best he could
>   With things not very subject to control,
> And turn'd, without perceiving his condition,
> Like Coleridge into a metaphysician.
>
>   .   .   .   .   .   .
>
> In thoughts like these true wisdom may discern
>   Longings sublime, and aspirations high,
> Which some are born with, but the most part learn
>   To plague themselves withal, they know not why:
> 'Twas strange that one so young should thus concern
>   His brain about the action of the sky;
> If *you* think 'twas philosophy that this did,
> I can't help thinking puberty assisted.

The satire is upon poets and human youth. It also builds up, more self-consciously than the satires of Pope or Dryden, the character of the speaker. But, as in *The Dunciad*, the poet always assumes his work to be literary, and he takes great pains to describe the qualities his epic poem must have. Even if he chooses to violate most of the epic conventions he knows he is doing so and therefore attaches his poem to the conventions by opposition and inversion.

The two kinds of satire I have mentioned might well be called the social and the expressive. These are not exclusive of each other

but mixed, the neoclassic tendency being toward the social. Both
kinds tend toward poetry's outer edge, since both seem to propose
as a primary interest direct comment upon living people or so-
cieties at a specific historical moment. In recent times satire has
tended to appear in prose fiction rather than in poetry, for reasons
which may become more apparent in Chapter 8.

Many verse satires are narratives. What we have noticed about
satires like "Absalom and Achitophel" and Don Juan is true also
of more solemn narrative verse: the neoclassic is social, the romantic personal. The story of action has become the province of
prose fiction. Sir Walter Scott was more successful in his prose
romances than his romantic narrative poems. More recently John
Masefield and E. J. Pratt have succeeded in poems where the story
is the thing, but they are the exceptions to the rule of prose.

VII

The eighteenth century did not, of course, invent the epistle and
the occasional poem. They are classic forms. But their outwardness
fitted the neoclassic interest. In his book on Dryden, Mark Van
Doren describes several kinds of epistles and complimentary addresses: First, the Horatian or didactic sort, which appears with
Daniel, proceeds to Drayton, Donne, Jonson, and Pope; second,
the Ovidian or "voluptuous," which culminates in Pope's "Eloisa
and Abelard"; third, the complimentary, which begins with Jonson,
proceeds through Waller and Cowley to Dryden.

Dryden was master of this last sort in an age that produced
much such verse. Van Doren describes him as a "large poet writing
largely about medium things," and this is a fair estimate.[1] Within
the bounds of the epistle, he can praise, describe, teach, and even
condense the history of poetry into a few heroic couplets, as in his
lines praising the Earl of Roscommon. Dryden was a great writer
of verse prologues and epilogues for plays by other playwrights.
These poems usually outshone the plays themselves in literary art,
and this suggests that the occasional poem directed upon an out-

[1] Mark Van Doren, John Dryden, Bloomington, 1960, p. 108.

ward moment can have its own inward integrity. Dryden's poems of this sort are too long to be quoted here, but a few can be named: The poem to Congreve on the occasion of his comedy, *The Double-Dealer;* "To Sir Godfrey Kneller"; "To My Honored Kinsman." The best of Dryden's prologues and epilogues are full of Dryden's own criticism of the drama, so that they become verse essays; and often they make witty attacks on critics, audiences, and fools, and become satires.

For Dryden it was not a great step from the verse essay, the epistle, the prologue and epilogue to the elegy. The elegy is in subject an occasional poem lamenting the death of a distinguished person or a friend, be he distinguished or not. It is also a poem of established conventions which even one of the most revolutionary of poets found difficult, indeed impossible, to escape. Frye's *Anatomy of Criticism* points out that Walt Whitman, who rejected Greek mythology and much poetic convention, nevertheless wrote a recognizable elegy on the death of Lincoln: ". . . he was right, being the kind of poet he was, in making the content of his own *When Lilacs Last in the Dooryard Bloomed* an elegy on Lincoln instead of a conventional Adonis lament. Yet his elegy is, in its *form,* as conventional as *Lycidas,* complete with purple flowers thrown on coffins, a great star drooping in the west, imagery of 'ever-returning spring' and all the rest of it. Poetry organizes the content of the world as it passes before the poet, but the forms in which that content is organized come out of the structure of poetry itself." [2] This is precisely why Dryden's great elegy "To the Memory of Mr. Oldham" is contemporary today, even though Oldham and Dryden have both been dead two centuries and Oldham mainly forgotten outside of a poem which has assimilated him to its form:

> Farewell, too little and too lately known,
> Whom I began to think and call my own:
> For sure our Souls were near alli'd, and thine
> Cast in the same poetick mold with mine.
> One common Note on either Lyre did strike,

[2] *Anatomy of Criticism,* Princeton, 1957, p. 102.

And Knaves and Fools we both abhorr'd alike.
To the same Goal did both our Studies drive:
The last set out the soonest did arrive.
Thus *Nisus* fell upon the slippery place,
Whilst his young Friend perform'd and won the Race.
O early ripe! to thy abundant Store
What could advancing Age have added more?
It might (what Nature never gives the Young)
Have taught the Numbers of thy Native Tongue.
But Satire needs not those, and Wit will shine
Through the harsh Cadence of a rugged Line.
A noble Error, and but seldom made,
When Poets are by too much force betray'd.
Thy gen'rous Fruits, though gather'd ere their prime,
Still shew'd a Quickness; and maturing Time
But mellows what we write to the dull Sweets of Rhyme.
Once more, hail, and farewell! farewell, thou young,
But ah! too short, *Marcellus* of our Tongue!
Thy Brows with Ivy and with Laurels bound;
But Fate and gloomy Night encompass thee around.

Van Doren has said of this poem that it is artificial, full of literary echoes, without an original word in the whole piece. It is almost a feat of memory in which Dryden's classical reading bubbled to his mind's surface.[3] But it is not a work of the fancy alone. It is a composition in which the parts, unexciting as parts, make a whole both aesthetically arresting and moving. With this poem as evidence we can conclude that the direction of all great poetry is ultimately inward toward the creation of its own verbal universe, from which the poet freely comments upon the other universes which man has created around him.

Some Suggested Reading

Frye, Northrop, *Anatomy of Criticism*, pp. 71–82.
Van Doren, Mark, *John Dryden, A Study of his Poetry*.
Willey, Basil, *The Eighteenth Century Background*.
[3] *Op. cit.*, p. 125.

6

Ode:

CLASSIC AND ROMANTIC

Keats: sonnet to ode, withdrawal from formal rigidity. Classical ode: Pindaric, Horatian, Anacreontic. Cowley's inventions. Romantic expressiveness traced from Gray. Philosophical and scientific influences. Shelley's "West Wind," Keats' negative capability, his sensuousness, "Ode to a Nightingale." Tate's "Ode to the Confederate Dead," his rejection of didacticism and expressivism. The poem as object.

1

John Keats (1795–1821), one of the best known English sonneteers, wrote more than sixty sonnets, but his handful of odes made his reputation. One critic of Keats, M. R. Ridley, has argued that Keats' development can be traced through the sonnets to the odes, in which form he seemed more at ease.[1] Allen Tate also takes note of this development: ". . . his experiments with the sonnet led him to modifications of the form which gave us the great stanzas of the Grecian Urn and Nightingale. And within that narrow, lyrical, and potentially dramatic compass he had something ready to say that he could not have said in the other kinds of verse that he had tried." [2] A glance at Keats' career as a sonnet-writer supports this. His first sonnet, "On Peace," is irregular in rime scheme. All the sonnets written from December, 1814 to January,

[1] *Keats' Craftsmanship*, Oxford, 1933.
[2] "A Reading of Keats," *On the Limits of Poetry*, New York, 1948, p. 169.

121

1818 (forty in number) are Italian. Thence onward to 1819, Keats experimented with Shakespearean, Italian, and irregular forms. The direction is obviously toward looseness. His famous sonnet "To Sleep" is one of the irregular sonnets:

O soft embalmer of the still midnight,	a
Shutting, with careful fingers and benign,	b
Our gloom-pleas'd eyes, embower'd from the light,	a
Enshaded in forgetfulness divine;	b
O soothest Sleep! if so it please thee, close	c 5
In midst of this thine hymn, my willing eyes,	d
Or wait the Amen, ere thy poppy throws	c
Around my bed its lulling charities;	d
Then save me, or the passed day will shine	b
Upon my pillow, breeding many woes;	c 10
Save me from curious conscience, that still lords	e
Its strength for darkness, burrowing like a mole;	f
Turn the key deftly in the oiled wards,	e
And seal the hushed casket of my soul.	f

The poem begins as a Shakespearean sonnet, but with line 9, it picks up a rime from the first quatrain. The poem is full of alliteration and assonance, and one senses that Keats is probably more interested in the use of internal devices of sound to build up sensuous impressions than he is in the traditional sonnet structures. Examination of an early draft of the poem bears out this view. The poet moves through the first quatrains with ease, but he is unable to deal successfully with the last six lines:

    O soft embalmer of the still midnight
    Shutting with careful fingers and benign
    Our gloom-pleas'd eyes embowered from the light
    As wearisome as darkness is divine
    O soothest sleep, if so it please thee close   5
    Mine willing eyes in midst of this thine hymn
    Or wait the amen, ere thy poppy throws
    Its sweet death dews o'er every pulse and limb —
    Then shut the hushed Casket of my soul
    And turn the key round in the oiled wards   10

> And let it rest until the morn has stole
>   grey east's
> Bright tresses From the west's shuddering bourn.

It is typical of many of Keats' later sonnets that after about the first ten lines the form seems to burst apart. The last three lines above are probably as bad as any Keats ever wrote. His excision of them was certainly wise, and, indeed, all of his revisions right down to the substitution of "seal" for "shut" and "deftly" for "round" are excellent. Nevertheless, one can argue that the sonnet form has been slightly neutralized by the irregularity of the rime scheme. Lines 9–11 are somewhat weak, the images imprecise, the language trite.

I do not want to base too elaborate an argument on the evidence of one sonnet, but I think it is typical of Keats' sonnets that they seldom sustain themselves fully as sonnets through the final sestet. Is it coincidence that the typical stanzaic pattern of Keats' great odes is ten lines (*ababcdecde*, as in the "Nightingale")? Perhaps Keats' ode stanza was a loosening and shortening of the sonnet. Keats' own "On the Sonnet" suggest a certain dissatisfaction with the sonnet as a constraining form:

> If by dull rhymes our English must be chain'd,
>   And, like Andromeda, the Sonnet sweet
> Fetter'd, in spite of pained loveliness;
> Let us find out, if we must be constrain'd,
>   Sandals more interwoven and complete   5
> To fit the naked foot of poesy;
> Let us inspect the lyre, and weigh the stress
> Of every chord, and see what may be gain'd
>   By ear industrious, and attention meet;
> Misers of sound and syllable no less   10
> Than Midas of his coinage, let us be
>   Jealous of dead leaves in the bay-wreath crown;
> So, if we may not let the Muse be free,
>   She will be bound with garlands of her own.

We must note that Keats is not an anti-formalist. Quite the contrary, he argues that the sonnet must never be an artificial constraint upon the poet's power to create form. This attitude can easily be squared with the presence of the ode as a kind of poem in which several eighteenth- and nineteenth-century poets excelled. One thinks of Gray's "On a Distant Prospect of Eton College" (1747), Collins' "Ode to Evening" (1746), and odes by Akenside, and the two Wartons. Among later poems, there are Wordsworth's "Intimations of Immortality," Shelley's "West Wind," and Coleridge's "France," to name only a few. It has been suggested that the ode, classical in its genesis, offered poets of this period an opportunity to withdraw from the rigidity of the heroic couplet and the dominant poetic tendencies of an "age of reason" into a kind of poem which allowed for a freer play of emotion and self-expression. The ode was a poem in which the poet discovered his form as he wrote. One finds these qualities in the odes of the later poets if not always in those of the earlier. Even in a poem as conventional and declamatory as Gray's "Eton College," one senses a personal involvement of feelings different from that of Dryden's or Pope's verse essays:

> Ah, happy hills! ah, pleasing shade!
> Ah, fields belov'd in vain!
> Where once my careless childhood stray'd,
> A stranger yet to pain!
> I feel the gales that from ye blow
> A momentary bliss bestow,
> As waving fresh their gladsome wing,
> My weary soul they seem to soothe,
> And, redolent with joy and youth,
> To breathe a second spring.

Although the ode can be roughly described as a poem in praise of something, it is not a poem of a particular verse form, or rime scheme, or subject. Nor does it demand a specific approach to a subject. In every age it has been adapted to the interests of individual poets. This very fact must have appealed to the romantic poets, revolutionary in attitude and method. In the changes in the ode itself are reflected the changes from classic to romantic taste.

11

Even before the romantics the English ode was a poem of great variety. This is partially because in classical literature three different kinds of poems were called odes. Pindaric odes, written by the poet Pindar, who lived at Thebes in the fifth century B.C., have had perhaps the greatest influence on English poetry. Most of his best known odes were written to commemorate the victory of some competitor in the Pythian or Olympian games. In the introduction to his translations of Pindar, Richmond Lattimore remarks that the modern reader may be surprised that such events should inspire poetry of a high order. No one has yet sung the prowess of Eddie Arcaro or even Bob Mathias. The Greek games were held in honor of the gods, on holy ground: "Further, success meant a demonstration of wealth and power (particularly in the chariot races) or of superb physical prowess, shown through peaceful and harmless means. The very uselessness of these triumphs . . . attracted Pindar. A victory meant that time, expense, and hard work had been lavished on an achievement which brought no calculable advantage, only honor and beauty. This may sound somewhat romantic, but competition symbolized an idea of nobility which meant much to Pindar; and in the exaltation of victory he seems sometimes to see a kind of transfiguration, briefly making radiant a world which most of the time seemed to him as to his contemporaries, dark and brutal." [3] This momentous sense of radiance, if nothing else, seems to be the abiding quality of the ode as it is transformed by the romantics into a personal, expressive poem.

Pindar's odes were evidently sometimes commissioned by the victor; even thoughts and names to be included may have been part of the contract. Generally the ode contained invocation, praise of the victor, reference (sometimes quite oblique and, to modern readers, obscure) to some suitable myth, and philosophical considerations. The form was never rigid, and the poet's aim was evidently to give the sense that his whole poem grew organically out of the event it was to praise. The Eighth Pythian Ode, for example

[3] *The Odes of Pindar*, Chicago, 1959, p. viii.

(a tribute to one Aristomones for having won at wrestling), begins
with an invocation of the goddess of peace, proceeds to a discussion of how "violence and high vaunting fail at the last," includes
references to mythical persons, and ends as follows (the translation
is Lattimore's):

> And above four bodies you threw
> your weight and your rage.
> To these lads was ordained
> At the Pythiad no delightful homefaring,
> nor, as they came to their mothers, did laughter break sweetly
>   about them
> to stir delight. Down back ways, avoiding mockers,
> they skulk, all stricken with their sad fortune.
>
> But he that has won some new
> splendor, in high pride
> of hope rides the air
> on the wings of his man's strength, and keeps
> desire beyond his wealth. In brief space mortals'
> delight is exalted, and thus again it drops to the ground,
> shaken by a backward doom.
>
> We are things of a day. What are we? What are we not?
>   The shadow of a dream
> is man, no more. But when the brightness comes, and God
>   gives it,
> there is a shining of light on men, and their life is sweet.
> Aigina, dear mother, bring this city to haven
> in free guise, by Zeus' aid and strong Aikos',
> Peleus and goodly Telamon aiding, and with Achilles.

The odes of Pindar were usually written in "triads" composed of
two stanzas called "strophe" and "antistrophe" and followed by
an "epode," different in shape. This form was derived from Greek
drama, but it was not until the romantics that the ode became
dramatic in itself rather than declamatory.

The second kind of classical ode was that of Horace, the Latin
poet. His odes were mainly monostrophic or composed of any number of stanzas, all of the same shape. Carol Maddison has described

them as follows: "In sum, the Horatian Ode is a relatively short poem usually written in quatrains, addressed to a friend, and containing moral or political reflections, commemorated largely by means of images and aphorisms." [4] Andrew Marvell's "An Horatian Ode upon Cromwell's Return from Ireland" exemplifies the adoption of several of these characteristics. Its stanza is the quatrain, its subject politics, its nature reflective (though also argumentative), and its ideas expressed through imagery. Two stanzas:

> So restless Cromwell could not cease
> In the inglorious arts of peace,
>   But through adventurous war
>   Urgèd his active star;
>
> And, like the three-forked lightning, first
> Breaking the clouds where it was nursed,
>   Did thorough his own side
>   His fiery way divide.

A third type of ode, named for the classical poet Anacreon (about whose actual existence there is doubt), need not detain us long. It is exemplified best by some of Robert Herrick's lyric poems. It is usually a short lyric on a light, often sensual subject. The poems attributed to Anacreon praise wine, women, and song. In almost every aspect their relation to the later English ode is in the name only. That all three kinds were accepted as odes by English renaissance taste, however, is demonstrated by Michael Drayton: "An ode is known to have been properly a Song. . . . They are (as the Learned say) divers: Some transcendently loftie, and farre more high than the Epick (commonly called the Heroique Poem) witnesse those of the inimitable Pindarus, consecrated to the glorie and renowne of such as returned in triumph from Olympus, Elis, Isthmus, or the like. Others, among the Greeks are amorous, soft, and made for Chambers, as other for Theaters; as were Anacreon's, the very Delicacies of the Grecian Erato. . . . Of a mixed kind were Horaces." [5]

[4] *Apollo and the Nine*, Baltimore, 1960, p. 33.
[5] Quoted in *Apollo and the Nine*, p. 291.

III

The typical English ode takes something from both the Pindaric and Horatian traditions as they developed in renaissance Europe. Abraham Cowley's so-called "Pindaric odes" were not really like Pindar's but instead irregular in form like Wordsworth's "Intimations of Immortality." They were generally, however, elevated and formal, public and rhetorical. Cowley wrote in the tradition of metaphysical wit (one of his odes is actually titled "On Wit") with logic as part of the poetic structure. He desired to appear enthused and inspired by his subject and to create a similar response in the reader. Instead of the mythological references of Pindar, Cowley, characteristically metaphysical, offers scientific and scholastic speculations of all sorts. Whether Cowley "misunderstood" the Pindaric ode, as Allen Tate and others have suggested, or was simply embarking from it is a question we need not consider. We can see that his use of the ode sets the stage for the later developments.

The appeal to the audience's enthusiasm and the irregular stanzaic pattern, suggestive of directly expressed inspiration, are typical results of romantic theories of art. Romantic odes have been aptly called odes of "passionate meditation." The speaker of the classic ode is essentially detached from his poem, as if he were its efficient cause. Pindar's Eighth Pythian Ode begins with an invocation to the goddess Hesychia, but it is not spoken in the poet's name. The poet acts as a kind of priest. Throughout his poem he does not intrude his own personality. True, he mentions himself, but the "I" of the poem is engaged only in formal gestures:

> In my haste I cannot lay
> leisure of long-drawn speech
>
> . . . I gaze in wonder and see plain
>
> . . . And I also take joy
> to cast a garland.

In John Milton's great ode, "On the Morning of Christ's Nativity," the "I" does not enter the poem even at these formal moments.

Nor does it in Marvell. Cowley rarely allows it to enter, and then only as part of a formal gesture, as in the poem on Crashaw:

> Pardon, my *Mother Church*, if I consent
> That *Angels* led him when from thee he went.

In the eighteenth century the poem's speaker occasionally took a somewhat larger role. This is evident in Gray's "Eton College," already mentioned, where the speaker associates the scene before him directly with the experiences of childhood. He is launched into a meditation upon lost innocence and inevitable death. Through the early evocation of childhood memory, the poem has a slightly personal twist. In Milton the poet seems only the medium of expression.

If we go back to Aristotle's definition of tragedy we see that there is no mention whatever of the poet's expressing himself or his feelings: "Tragedy, then, is an imitation of an action that is serious, complete, and of a certain magnitude, in language embellished with each kind of artistic ornament, the several kinds being found in separate parts of the play; in the form of action, not of narrative; through pity and fear effecting the proper purgation of these emotions." We are not, of course, concerned with drama here, nor was Aristotle concerned with the ode-like choruses of Greek tragedy; nevertheless the order of importance which he suggests is instructive to us as students of the classical temper. The work of art is assumed to be primarily an "imitation," to be oriented toward the world around us. Second, it must affect the audience. No mention at all is made of the poet's relation to the work of art. The poet would seem to be important primarily as the vessel through which the work passes. Perhaps the classical invocation of the muses at the outset of so many odes indicates that the reader should look away from the author. As far back as Homer, who asks for the muse's aid in telling his great stories, the poet is the muse's priest. If the romantic poets associated inspiration with the power to express the self, the classical and neoclassical poets associated it with the power to affect the audience through a just representation of events. Even when Cowley suggested exuberance it was not in order to open his heart but to affect the audience with elevated sentiments.

In Gray's "Eton College" we detect a tendency to turn inward. This tendency is even more pronounced in Collins' "Ode to Evening." The "I" is in neither case a key figure in the poem, but the descriptions of nature are not so objectively conceived as they often are in the neoclassic ode. Collins' poem is an invocation to the goddess of evening, combined with descriptions. No longer is the invocation purely a formal rite through and beyond which the poem moves. One senses the speaker personally straining after identification with evening itself. The poet seems to put himself in direct relation to the objects he describes; the descriptions are more sensuous and particular than we are likely to find in Gray or Akenside or other poets of the time.

This movement toward the subjective gains momentum in the romantic period, where the poet turns away from classical "imitation." For Coleridge art was the inner made outer. For Wordsworth it was the "spontaneous overflow of powerful feelings," and the poet was not simply a vessel or mirror held up to nature but a fountain and a "man speaking to men." In Wordsworth's famous Preface, he regards actions described in poems as having for their purpose the expression of feeling. The feelings are not there to express the actions. Keats' subjectivity expresses itself in his well-known remark, "O for a life of Sensations rather than of Thoughts."

The reasons for this shift from neoclassic "reason" to romantic "imagination" are complex. Wordsworth was reacting, as we saw in Chapter 2, against a worn-out poetic diction. He sought a basis for a new diction in his appeal to sincerity, to naturalness of feeling and speech. The turning inward to self-expression had deeper sources, however. It was involved with the birth of psychology as a formal study, with the emphasis upon epistemology in philosophy, and with surging individualism in politics and economics. Indeed, everything in the age pointed to the individual.

In philosophy the rise of science saw the perceptual world divided into subjective and objective realms. Science posited a

mechanical world of physical forces. Reality in such
reduced to that which is measurable. The criterion of all
upon reality was, on this basis, quantitative and materialis
philosopher John Locke (1632–1704) had formalized the
tive-subjective opposition by drawing his distinction between
"primary" and "secondary" qualities of experience. The "primary
qualities were those which exist in the so-called "outer" world —
weight, mass, extension, etc. (all the measurable qualities). The
"secondary" qualities were those which the human mind creates —
color, smell, texture, sound, etc. Science took as its realm the primary qualities, the measurable world, and it would seem that
poetry and art in general now had only secondary experience with
which to deal. There were, of course, critiques of Locke's "bifurca-
tion of nature" into two distinct realms. Bishop Berkeley, for one,
questioned whether if the secondary qualities are subjective, we
can ever know the primary world, since we perceive it only in the
form of the secondary qualities and must shakily infer the existence
of the primary. Kant's attempt to solve this dilemma was only one
of the efforts to escape the solipsism which seemed to develop
from a position such as Berkeley's (where every individual is apparently isolated within his own subjective experience); and yet
Kant sought to avoid Locke's relegation of secondary experience
to the meaningless.

Romantic poetry sought to assert the worth of unique individual
experience, the reality of the subjective world. It took a position
essentially anti-rationalistic insofar as rationalism suggests scientific
method operating upon a soundless, scentless, colorless universe,
"only the hurrying of matter, endlessly, meaninglessly," as the
twentieth-century philosopher A. N. Whitehead has described it.

It is hardly surprising in the light of these intellectual developments that the ode moved in the direction of the private, subjective, self-expressive meditation, with the poet himself at the center
of the experience. Nor is it surprising further that as soon as subjectivity becomes a dominant poetic situation, a major theme
among poets is how to escape the confines of the self and make a
relationship to something other than the self. In the Lockean sys-

nded by a prison of dead matter
ossible to "speak." He finds some-
bject to analysis and measurement.
such a world would be to weigh,
lesires a living, answering object.
must re-establish the qualities of
to the subjective. Nature must
..st be recognized as significant
experiences are real. They cannot be re-
on a graph or items leading to some sociological gen-
..alization. One of the period's best-known odes, Shelley's "Ode
to the West Wind," is a dramatic description of the effort to establish relation with some *other*, figured forth as the wind. The poet
attempts to marry his own inner being to something symbolic of
the whole of nature, which Shelley insists is alive, not dead as
materialistic analysis would have it.

The ode's beginning is, like Pindar's, an invocation, but as we
read on we discover that it is *all* invocation. In this it surpasses
Collins' "Ode to Evening." Shelley does not pause to meditate and
only briefly pauses to describe. He maintains direct address to the
wind throughout. The speaker's essential desire is for the wind to
hear, and he knows that the statement must be inspired enough
to succeed with this desire. By comparison Collins seems satisfied
to make his address and be done with it. In Shelley the traditional
invocation of the ode is transformed into an evocation and is extended through the poem to become its total structure:

> Wild spirit which art moving every where;
> Destroyer and preserver, hear, O hear!

But the speaker desires a certain *kind* of relationship. In the last
two sections of the poem two possible states of relation are suggested:

4.

> If I were a dead leaf thou mightest bear;
> If I were a swift cloud to fly with thee;
> A wave to pant beneath thy power and share

The impulse of thy strength, only less free
Than thou, O uncontroulable! If even
I were as in my boyhood, and could be

The comrade of thy wanderings over heaven,
As then, when to outstrip thy skiey speed
Scarce seemed a vision; I would ne'er have striven

As thus with thee in prayer in my sore need.
Oh! lift me as a wave, a leaf, a cloud!
I fall upon the thorns of life! I bleed!

A heavy weight of hours has chained and bowed
One too like thee: tameless, and swift, and proud.

5.

Make me thy lyre, even as the forest is:
What if my leaves are falling like its own!
The tumult of thy mighty harmonies

Will take from both a deep, autumnal tone,
Sweet though in sadness. Be thou, spirit fierce,
My spirit! Be thou me, impetuous one!

Drive my dead thoughts over the universe
Like withered leaves to quicken a new birth!
And, by the incantation of this verse,

Scatter, as from an unextinguished hearth
Ashes and sparks, my words among mankind!
Be through my lips to unawakened earth

The trumpet of a prophecy! O, Wind,
If Winter comes, can Spring be far behind?

In the fourth section submission to the wind's force seems to be
the height of desire, but this state is surpassed in the fifth section
in favor of a less passive condition represented by the forest, seen
as a gigantic wind harp. In the wind harp, or aeolian lyre, the romantic poets saw an image of the mind's relation to natural
phenomena. Coleridge wrote a poem entitled "The Aeolian Harp."
Wordsworth employed the image, and Shelley refers to it in his
"Defense of Poetry" as follows:

Man is an instrument over which a series of external and internal impressions are driven, like the alternations of an ever-changing wind over an Aeolian lyre, which move it by their motion to ever-changing melody. But there is a principle within the human being, and perhaps within all sentient beings, which acts otherwise than in the lyre, and produces not melody, alone, but harmony, by an internal adjustment of the sounds or motions thus excited to the impressions which excite them. It is as if the lyre could accommodate its chords to the motions of that which strikes them. . . .[6]

Here, of course, Shelley ultimately discards the lyre image as not quite adequate to represent the relation of inner to outer world. It makes the inner world seem too passive a receptacle. Nevertheless, in his ode the figure represents an active marriage between wind and speaker — objective nature and subjective mind, with neither side a passive recipient of experience. The poet is no longer the leaf but the tree from which the leaves fall; and the leaves are his own completed poems scattered through civilization to demonstrate that the rebirth of man's imaginative life is possible. For Shelley, reality is neither subjective and imprisoned within man nor objective Lockean matter. It is instead the imaginative *relation* of man to nature. The final image of the ode, the "unextinguished hearth," is similar to that of the lyre, and it too has its counterpart in the "Defense":

The mind in creation is as a fading coal, which some invisible influence, like an inconstant wind, awakens to transitory brightness; this power arises from within, like the colour of a flower which fades and changes as it is developed.

This image the poet is careful to make more active and creative than the aeolian lyre. Its power comes from within. It is one that Coleridge would have applauded as nearly adequate to a description of the "shaping spirit of imagination," that power in man which gives to the universe meaning beyond measurement.

[6] *Selected Poetry and Prose* (K. N. Cameron, ed.), New York, 1951, pp. 482–483.

IV

We may now finally return to Keats, with whom we began. In a letter of 1817, Keats made a distinction which pervades his idea of poetry:

> . . . I have never yet been able to perceive how any thing can be known for truth by consequitive reasoning — and yet it must be. Can it be that even the greatest Philosopher ever arrived at his goal without putting aside numerous objections? However it may be, O for a Life of Sensations rather than of Thoughts! [7]

For Keats, "thought" meant the analytic, measuring, categorizing power of the mind. In his famous "Ode on a Grecian Urn," he asserts that the urn, an object of little interest except as a container to this kind of mental power, "dost tease us out of thought," simply because "thought," as he uses the term, is inadequate to our experience of the urn. The urn entices us to surrender our aloof analytic tendency. We are invited to confront the urn with other mental powers. This other way of experience Keats calls (above) the "life of sensations." One should not confuse his statement with a cry in favor of sheer hedonistic pleasure. Instead we should read it as a plea against the Lockean distinction between subject and object. Keats refuses to make the sensuous or "secondary" experience of touch, taste, smell, color, etc., merely subjective and valueless. Instead he finds value only in experience which includes them. He rejects the "truth" of a thinker who abstracts a soundless, scentless, colorless "reality" from immediate experience. This is one reason for the heavy emphasis upon sensuous detail in Keats' odes. Truth exists only where sensation contributes to reality. Keats' marriage of the self and nature or the *other* occurs through the imaginative identification of the feelings with the object:

> As to the poetical Character itself . . . it is not itself — it has no self — it is every thing and nothing — It has no character — it enjoys light and shade; it lives in gusto, be it foul or fair, high or

[7] *Selected Poetry and Letters* (R. H. Fogle, ed.), New York, 1951, p. 301.

low, rich or poor, mean or elevated — It has as much delight in conceiving an Iago as an Imogen. What shocks the virtuous philosopher delights the camelion poet. . . . A poet is the most unpoetical of any thing in existence; because he has no Identity — he is continually informing — and filling some other body.[8]

The richness, the tapestry-like quality of Keats' poetry is the result of a single-minded application of these ideas to poetic technique. Typical are the first four lines of "Ode to a Nightingale":

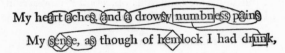

My heart aches, and a drowsy numbness pains

My sense, as though of hemlock I had drunk,

Or emptied some dull opiate to the drains

One minute past, and Lethe-wards had sunk.

The play with vowels and soft consonants is very complex and intensified. I have marked only a few of the relationships in lines 1 and 2. The same sounds are extended and manipulated through lines 3 and 4. I have not marked the dominant alliteration: "drowsy," "drunk," "dull," "drains." Some of these words are interlocked with the rime scheme — "drains-pains," "drunk-sunk," which in turn relates them to the repetition of the soft consonant "n" through the whole quatrain. Also related in this network of rime, alliteration, and assonance is the play with the various "a" sounds. The quatrain has a strong sensuous impact.

The stanza proceeds:

'Tis not through envy of thy happy lot,
But being too happy in thine happiness, —
That thou, light-winged Dryad of the trees,
In some melodious plot
Of beechen green, and shadows numberless,
Singest of summer in full-throated ease.

The syntax is somewhat bothersome because it is condensed. The sense is: My heart aches because I have heard your song, not be-

8 *Ibid.*, p. 320.

cause I envy your happy lot but because I suffer a surfeit of happiness when, in a sort of empathy, I experience your happiness.

The poem proceeds through a spectacular series of synæsthetic images and proposes that the speaker might like to "leave the world unseen" by drinking a wine which embodies the finest qualities of its pastoral source:

> O, for a draught of vintage! that hath been
>   Cool'd a long age in the deep-delved earth,
> Tasting of Flora and the country green,
>   Dance, and Provençal song, and sunburnt mirth!
> O for a beaker full of the warm South,
>   Full of the true, the blushful Hippocrene,
>   With beaded bubbles winking at the brim,
>   And purple-stained mouth;
>   That I might drink, and leave the world unseen,
>   And with thee fade away into the forest dim:

But the poet rejects wine in favor of imaginative flight, which is really his main concern. Wine is an instrument of passivity, ultimately a depressant. And the poet clearly, from the third stanza wishes to escape the depression of a world in which man, devoid of imaginative power, seeing his life only as a diminishing measurable entity, awaits only his material demise:

> Fade far away, dissolve, and quite forget
>   What thou among the leaves hast never known,
> The weariness, the fever, and the fret
>   Here, where men sit and hear each other groan;
> Where palsy shakes a few, sad, last gray hairs,
>   Where youth grows pale, and spectre-thin, and dies;
>   Where but to think is to be full of sorrow
>   And leaden-eyed despairs,
>   Where Beauty cannot keep her lustrous eyes,
>   Or new Love pine at them beyond to-morrow.

> Away! away! for I will fly with thee,
>   Not charioted by Bacchus and his pards,
> But on the viewless wings of Poesy,
>   Though the dull brain perplexes and retards:
> Already with thee! tender is the night,

> And haply the Queen-Moon is on her throne,
>> Cluster'd around by all her starry Fays;
>>> But here there is no light,
>> Save what from heaven is with the breezes blown
>>> Through verdurous glooms and winding mossy ways.

But to raise oneself above the materialistic view of human nature is not easy, and to sustain that position is even more difficult. The speaker cannot ultimately fly with the nightingale, and he falls from his imaginative flight. To him, the nightingale, not encumbered by "thought," incapable of reasoning upon its own future and thus unaware of death, lacking self-consciousness, unable to measure time or measure anything, is in a sense deathless. The nightingale is thus the same bird which Keats imagines sang for the Biblical Ruth and will sing again for future generations. The human being's unique predicament is that, capable of reason, he is also capable of a torturing awareness of devouring time, of himself as a natural being, of his own ephemeral nature. He is caught between imagination and reason, "sensation" (the nightingale's world) and "thought" (the world of knowledge).

In the last stanza Keats bids adieu to the nightingale, saddened by the failure of his fancy to transport him fully from the confines of his own ego. His flight of fancy has been hauled back to earth ironically by the very language he employs to describe his experience. "Forlorn" recalls to him his imprisoned self. The speaker has momentarily accepted the materialistic premises, which make the fancy escapist and unrealistic. From this point of view the fancy is simply not strong enough to obliterate reality.

But as the poem ends, the speaker, moved by the intensity of his experience, is not quite willing to hold this position. He is no longer sure which of his worlds is real. He is not certain whether his hearing the nightingale occurred in a dream or whether he was then awake and is now asleep. Is the realm of reason and "thought" man's dream from which the nightingale momentarily awakened him? Perhaps.

> Thou wast not born for death, immortal Bird!
>> No hungry generations tread thee down;

The voice I hear this passing night was heard
   In ancient days by emperor and clown:
Perhaps the self-same song that found a path
   Through the sad heart of Ruth, when, sick for home,
      She stood in tears amid the alien corn;
         The same that oft-times hath
Charm'd magic casements, opening on the foam
   Of perilous seas, in faery lands forlorn.

Forlorn! the very word is like a bell
   To toll me back from thee to my sole self!
Adieu! the fancy cannot cheat so well
   As she is fam'd to do, deceiving elf.
Adieu! adieu! thy plaintive anthem fades
   Past the near meadows, over the still stream,
      Up the hill-side; and now 'tis buried deep
         In the next valley-glades:
   Was it a vision, or a waking dream?
      Fled is that music: — Do I wake or sleep?

Keats' ode ends with the final question unresolved. This may be annoying to the reader who desires the poem to reason discursively toward a definite answer to the problems it poses. I remind such a reader of the lines already quoted from Stauffer's "The Lemmings":

> After all, reflective verse shouldn't give the answers.
> It should merely set the questions moving like dancers.

As an art the dance does not speak to us. With this image we return to the idea of the poem as an object, like the urns and nightingales within Keats' poems.

Keats, himself, put it best when he described what is necessary to the artist:

> . . . it struck me what quality went to form a Man of Achievement, especially in Literature, and which Shakespeare possessed so enormously — I mean *Negative Capability*, that is, when a man is capable of being in uncertainties, mysteries, doubts, without any irritable reaching after fact and reason.[9]

This view of the artist allows for a conception of the poem as an artifice, not necessarily concerned with communicating an idea.

[9] *Ibid.*, p. 304.

Keats was opposed to the sort of poetry which makes dogmatic assertions:

> . . . for the sake of a few fine imaginative or domestic passages, are we to be bullied into a certain Philosophy engendered in the whims of an Egotist? . . . We hate poetry that has a palpable design upon us.[10]

In spite of a dominant conception among the romantics of the poem as expressive of the poet's inner being, in most of Keats' odes we discover more than mere self-expression. The speaker, when successfully detached from the poet's whims and dogmatisms, becomes the main character in the poem's drama. "Ode to a Nightingale" is dramatic, even though drama in this instance exists in the speaker's mind. Just as we need not accept any of Hamlet's statements as true outside the confines of the play, so too in Keats' poem we need not discover any conceptual statement which tells us what the poem means. The poem gives us the drama of meditation, reflection, and sensation.

It is said that the ode as practiced by Pindar originated as a choral song in Greek drama. The odes of Keats are the whole of a drama, not a part; they are also personal and interior dramas rather than public ones, as were Pindar's. But just as the Greek chorus sings meaningfully only within the meaning of the whole play, so does Keats' speaker exist only in the world the poem has created. In such a poem romantic *subjectivity* creates a poetic *object*.

V

One of the most interesting odes of recent times is Allen Tate's "Ode to the Confederate Dead." Since Tate has been unsympathetic to romanticism in general (though friendly to Keats), it is interesting to see that his ode has some things in common with the romantic ode. In an essay on his poem, entitled "Narcissus as Narcissus," Tate acknowledges the "subjectivity" of his ode:

[10] *Ibid.*, p. 406.

I have been asked why I called the poem an ode. I first called it an elegy. It is an ode only in the sense in which Cowley in the seventeenth century misunderstood the real structure of the Pindaric ode. Not only are meter and rhyme without fixed pattern, but in another feature the poem is even further removed from Pindar than Abraham Cowley was: a purely subjective meditation would not even in Cowley's age have been called an ode.[11]

Then, avoiding the obvious resemblance to the romantic ode, probably because of his well advertised dislike of certain romantic excesses, he goes on:

I suppose in so calling it, I intended an irony: the scene of the poem is not a public celebration, it is a lone man at a gate.

Of course, no ode of Pindar contained as its scene a celebration. It was, all of it, *part* of a celebration. Tate is simply assuming here that a poem *contains* a scene, is a kind of drama. "Figure to yourself," he says, "a man stopping at the gate of a Confederate graveyard on a late autumn afternoon. The leaves are falling; his first impressions bring him the 'rumor of mortality.' . . ." He is telling us that we must infer the stage setting and then listen in on the meditation of the actor:

Row after row with strict impunity
The headstones yield their names to the elements,
The wind whirrs without recollection.

Tate also takes pains to reject all possibility that we read the poem as anything but dramatic. The poem *tells* us nothing, makes no "palpable demands" upon us. Nor can we complain if the poem rejects what we naïvely call reality:

. . . the sea boils and pigs have wings because in poetry all things are possible — if you are man enough. They are possible because in poetry the disparate elements are not combined in logic, which can join things only under certain categories and under the law of contradiction; they are combined in poetry rather as experience, and experience has decided to ignore logic, except perhaps as another field of experience. Experience means conflict, our natures being what they are, and conflict means drama.

[11] *On the Limits of Poetry*, p. 256.

In Tate's conception, then, his ode is not the "spontaneous over-flow of powerful feelings." It has an objective structure, and its subjectivity is that of the man at the gate, not Tate himself. Nor does Tate conceive of the poem as a communication with the reader. The poem was much revised, not he says, "for the convenience of the reader, but for the poem's own clarity, so that word, phrase, line, passage, the poem might at worst come near its best expression."

One may ask whether the reader's convenience and the poem's own clarity are necessarily at odds. Not necessarily, we can assume, but it is quite possible that they *may* be. It is unlikely that a good poem will do more than confuse a blockhead. The poet still writes to a muse representing artistic perfection rather than to a reader chosen at random. In any case, Tate wishes to prevent his reader from assuming that he should read the poem to find out about Allen Tate, which is the logical conclusion one draws from the expressive theory of art. Such a theory leads to our interest in reconstructing the poet's inner life from the evidence of the poems, on the assumption that we are thereby brought into relation with a great soul. In all this, the poem as an artifice is forgotten.

Tate wishes also to make the reader forget about extracting some paraphrasable "content" from his poem. It is not crudely didactic. Rejecting both neoclassical didacticism and romantic expressivism, Tate insists upon the poem as an objective thing. It is interesting that Tate conceives of his poem as concerned with the very question that the development of the ode has raised:

> The poem is "about" solipsism, a philosophical doctrine which says that we create the world in the act of perceiving it, or about Narcissism, or any other *ism* that denotes the failure of the human personality to function objectively in nature and society.

Tate thus reasserts the ode's interest in external reality while at the same time he employs subjective meditation in his poem.

Some Suggested Reading

Abrams, M. H., *The Mirror and the Lamp, Romantic Theory and the Critical Tradition.*

Bate, Walter J., *From Classic to Romantic.*

Gleckner, Robert F., and Enscoe, Gerald E. (editors), *Romanticism: Points of View.*

Lattimore, Richmond (translator), *The Odes of Pindar.*

Maddison, Carol, *Apollo and the Nine, A History of the Ode.*

Shafer, Robert, *The English Ode to 1660.*

Shuster, George N., *The English Ode from Milton to Keats.*

Tate, Allen, "A Reading of Keats" and "Narcissus as Narcissus" in *On the Limits of Poetry.*

7 Dramatic Monologue:

DRAMA INTO CHARACTER

Romantic subjectivity and dramatic objectivity: the character's, not the poet's subjectivity. Inference in Browning's "My Last Duchess." Drama as it reveals character. Contrast to the soliloquy: Hamlet. Tone and statement in Tennyson. Inner monologues: Browning and Eliot. Monologue in modern fiction. The dramatic in modern poetry: Yeats.

1

In one of his letters Keats wrote: "If a Sparrow come before my window I take part in its existence and pick about the Gravel." This principle of empathy in Keats moves curiously in the direction of dramatic detachment from the self ("negative capability" as I have described it in Chapter 6). The tendency of the Keatsian ode was dramatic, but it was an inner sort of drama, most of the action taking place on the stage of the speaker's mind. After the romantic emphasis upon the inner world and the poem as an expression of the poet's self, the problem of poets was to regain some of the freedom lost by this romantic subjectivity. Keats' principle of empathy suggests a way out of the ego's enclosure into other objects, even (as he once said) inanimate things like billiard balls. Past these empathetic identifications comes detachment: a dominant form to arise was the dramatic monologue. But the purpose of the dramatic monologue was still to express the inner life. This inner life was no longer, however, the poet's own. It was clearly

144

that of a speaker not the poet. No one, we hope, confuses Browning's Duke in "My Last Duchess" with the author. That poem appears at first as a slice out of a play with all the speaking parts except the Duke's erased. And yet there is no such play and never was. What Browning's poem gives to us is all that is necessary to his purpose. He is not interested in a drama which presents significant actions as more important than the characters engaged in them. He is concerned first and last with the projection of one character's essential *being*. He therefore chooses an episode which epitomizes that being. It need not be very long or even climactic or decisive in the character's life as long as it is characteristic. Unless the poem is an interior monologue, of which we shall later take note, we are supposed to make a mass of inferences from the scene played out before us. Only on its surface is the dramatic monologue locked in a particular moment or period of time. As a revelation of the speaker's being it has no real beginning or end but is the door to a large, mostly hidden room, the contents and the hidden dimensions of which we infer from looking through the door at what we *can* see. The speaker lives both before and after the events of the monologue (unless of course the scene is of the speaker's death), but these events epitomize that before and after, sometimes by suggesting and recalling those events but often simply by making us *know* the character. In fact, the past and future only enter as they bear directly upon the present action.

This almost exclusive interest in character rather than action identifies the dramatic monologue as an outgrowth of romantic subjectivity. In Wordsworth's statement that the action of his poem is presented to express the feelings, not vice versa, we need only to substitute character for feelings. The romantic poet's expressiveness becomes the expressiveness of a character in the poem:

> That's my last Duchess painted on the wall,
> Looking as if she were alive. I call
> That piece a wonder, now: Fra Pandolf's hands
> Worked busily a day, and there she stands.
> Will't please you sit and look at her? I said
> "Fra Pandolf" by design, for never read

Strangers like you that pictured countenance,
The depth and passion of its earnest glance,
But to myself they turned (since none puts by
The curtain I have drawn for you, but I)
And seemed as they would ask me, if they durst,
How such a glance came there; so, not the first
Are you to turn and ask thus. Sir, 'twas not
Her husband's presence only, called that spot
Of joy into the Duchess' cheek: perhaps
Fra Pandolf chanced to say "Her mantle laps
Over my lady's wrist too much," or "Paint
Must never hope to reproduce the faint
Half-flush that dies along her throat": such stuff
Was courtesy, she thought, and cause enough
For calling up that spot of joy. She had
A heart — how shall I say? — too soon made glad,
Too easily impressed; she liked whate'er
She looked on, and her looks went everywhere.
Sir, 'twas all one! My favour at her breast,
The dropping of the daylight in the West,
The bough of cherries some officious fool
Broke in the orchard for her, the white mule
She rode with round the terrace — all and each
Would draw from her alike the approving speech,
Or blush, at least. She thanked men, — good!
    but thanked
Somehow — I know not how — as if she ranked
My gift of a nine-hundred-years-old name
With anybody's gift. Who'd stoop to blame
This sort of trifling? Even had you skill
In speech — (which I have not) — to make your will
Quite clear to such an one, and say, "Just this
Or that in you disgusts me; here you miss,
Or there exceed the mark" — and if she let
Herself be lessoned so, nor plainly set
Her wits to yours, forsooth, and made excuse,
— E'en then would be some stooping; and I choose
Never to stoop. Oh sir, she smiled, no doubt,
Whene'er I passed her; but who passed without
Much the same smile? This grew; I gave commands;
Then all smiles stopped together. There she stands
As if alive. Will't please you rise? We'll meet

The company below, then. I repeat,
The Count your master's known munificence
Is ample warrant that no just pretence
Of mine for dowry will be disallowed;
Though his fair daughter's self, as I avowed
At starting, is my object. Nay, we'll go
Together down, sir. Notice Neptune, though,
Taming a sea-horse, thought a rarity,
Which Claus of Innsbruck cast in bronze for me!

Here we must infer a great deal from the words provided: the nature of the scene, the existence on the stage of another actor, the situations to which the Duke sometimes cryptically refers. The poet makes us reach decisions about what the Duke says and, ultimately, about what the Duke is. We must consider how and why the Duke has brought the Count's envoy before the picture. His manner is peculiarly offhand; but as he continues to speak we realize that much of what he says and does is ruthlessly contrived to impress the Count. Nevertheless, we suspect that the Duke has unwittingly revealed more than he means to have revealed about himself. Sometimes we are not sure just how far he has meant to go and are left trying to decide between two horrendous conclusions. We realize, of course, that his own jealousy, his monumental egoism, have led him too far. He has revealed an awful materialistic possessiveness. While she lived, he thought of the first Duchess merely as an object, and that she lives now only in the painting is apparently a convenience to him, for in real life she was a source of torment. He can now place her among his *objets d'art*. From the famous lines,

. . . This grew; I gave commands;
Then all smiles stopped together.

are we to infer that the Duke really did have his Duchess murdered for her "indiscretions"? Are we then to conclude that he has revealed, on the emotion of the moment, more than he meant to; or has his egoism driven him to a bald, quite unpremeditated confession in order to impress the Count and prospective bride with exactly how she must behave? Or is the oblique reference to the stopping of smiles meant only to leave the envoy not *quite* certain whether the lady was murdered or not, but certain enough of the Duke's ruthlessness to warn the Count about his daughter's future behavior? Or has the Duke for the same reason simply fabricated the illusion of murder? No matter how we decide, the Duke is revealed as cold, brutal, and egocentric. Observe what immediately follows:

> . . . There she stands
> As if alive.

No matter what the answer, the utter ruthlessness of these lines, coming after those previous, suggests that the Duke may be capable of the worst. It is not, then, so much what the Duke actually *did* as it is what he *is* that is revealed to us. It is often how he puts two statements together, how he can express *this* and with perfect coolness go on to *that* which reveals his nature.

It is perhaps a question just how much of himself the Duke is able to control. He may say what he wants to, but he may not be able to control the relation between his statements, and we may infer things about him. Or does he contrive these juxtapositions diabolically and then glory in what he has revealed of his power? The poem's ending is an example of this; the Duke has ostensibly been showing the envoy through his art collection. Even after he has completed his discussion of the Duchess he does not forget the formal occasion and coolly points out one final *objet d'art* as they descend. This puts the final touch upon the Duke's attitude toward his Duchess and places her squarely among his artifacts.

Because it constantly leads us to make inferences and because of its form, the poem is ambiguous. We feel drawn toward making decisions about actions and motives with only the evidence of the Duke's words. But as a revelation of being the poem is as direct as an exterior monologue can be. The Duke reveals himself directly. It is not his career that he reveals but his *being*. Action exists for the sake of the characterization.

The dramatic monologue is not really like any part of a play. Nor is it a play in itself. When we compare it to one of Hamlet's soliloquies, where one person speaks alone on the stage, we recognize that there is a great difference. Drama exists in the monologue, but the soliloquy exists in the drama. Let us examine for a moment one of Hamlet's soliloquies:

> O, what a rogue and peasant slave am I!
> Is it not monstrous that this player here,
> But in a fiction, in a dream of passion,
> Could force his soul so to his own conceit
> That, from her working, all his visage wann'd,
> Tears in his eyes, distraction in's aspect,
> A broken voice, and his whole function suiting
> With forms to his conceit? And all for nothing!
> For Hecuba!
> What's Hecuba to him, or he to Hecuba,
> That he should weep for her? What would he do,
> Had he the motive and the cue for passion
> That I have? He would drown the stage with tears
> And cleave the general ear with horrid speech;
> Make mad the guilty and appal the free,
> Confound the ignorant, and amaze indeed
> The very faculties of eyes and ears.
> Yet I,
> A dull and muddy-mettled rascal, peak
> Like John-a-dreams, unpregnant of my cause,
> And can say nothing! No, not for a king,
> Upon whose property and most dear life
> A damn'd defeat was made. Am I a coward?
> Who calls me villain? breaks my pate across?
> Plucks off my beard and blows it in my face?
> Tweaks me by th' nose? gives me the lie i'th'throat
> As deep as to the lungs? Who does me this, ha?
> 'Swounds, I should take it! for it cannot be
> But I am pigeon-liver'd and lack gall
> To make oppression bitter, or ere this
> I should have fatted all the region kites
> With this slave's offal. Bloody, bawdy villain!
> Remorseless, treacherous, lecherous, kindless villain!
> O, vengeance!
> Why, what an ass am I! This is most brave,
> That I, the son of a dear father murther'd,
> Prompted to my revenge by heaven and hell,

Must (like a whore) unpack my heart with words
And fall a-cursing like a very drab,
A scullion!
Fie upon't! foh! About, my brain! Hum, I have heard
That guilty creatures, sitting at a play,
Have by the very cunning of the scene
Been struck so to the soul that presently
They have proclaim'd their malefactions;
For murther, though it have no tongue, will speak
With most miraculous organ. I'll have these players
Play something like the murther of my father
Before mine uncle. I'll observe his looks;
I'll tent him to the quick. If he but blench,
I know my course. The spirit that I have seen
May be a devil; and the devil hath power
T'assume a pleasing shape; yea, and perhaps
Out of my weakness and my melancholy,
As he is very potent with such spirits,
Abuses me to damn me. I'll have grounds
More relative than this. The play's the thing
Wherein I'll catch the conscience of the King.

Although Hamlet works himself up to emotional heights, his speech is nevertheless an objective search into himself. In the Shakespearean soliloquy the speaker sees *himself*, usually quite accurately; in the dramatic monologue this revelation of the self to the self is usually lacking. Furthermore, the soliloquy is part of an action and furthers the plot, whereas the dramatic monologue gradually reveals what was already there. Hamlet moves from self-analysis to decision, and thus the soliloquy moves the play to its conclusion; but drama in the dramatic monologue is not, as Aristotle called drama, "an imitation of an action." It is the flowing-forth of character. Even where there is no appreciable development of action, as in Hamlet's "To be or not to be" soliloquy, the point is that Hamlet does not *act*; but the soliloquy is still conceived in terms of action and delay, as Hamlet's last lines amply testify:

Thus conscience does make cowards of us all,
And thus the native hue of resolution

Is sicklied o'er with the pale cast of thought,
And enterprises of great pith and moment
With this regard their currents turn awry
And lose the name of action.

Nor does Hamlet have any ulterior purpose in his speech. The difference betwen soliloquy and monologue is excellently described in Robert Langbaum's *The Poetry of Experience* in the following way: The soliloquist never tries to fool his audience, but is instead searching for the right attitude toward his situation. He seeks to render the situation objectively and is therefore freer to analyze himself and his position from the outside. The dramatic monologue's "I" is absorbed in his experience and is not trying to reveal himself to anyone not even himself. That he does after all, reveal himself is incidental to some other purpose. In fact, he may even be attempting to conceal his nature.[1] The essence of the dramatic monologue, then, lies in the speaker's relation to himself. In the dramatic monologue there is always something which the speaker does not necessarily mean to reveal.

No long speech in Shakespeare is a dramatic monologue. Antony's funeral oration over Caesar is full of ironies, but they are conscious ironies, and the speaker means what he says. He is not overheard, but heard directly. The speech's function in the play is to move the action and only secondarily to reveal Antony. Taken alone it might even mislead us about him. The dramatic monologue is unique in its containment of the drama of character.

II

It has been argued that in reading a dramatic monologue we clearly adopt the speaker's point of view as the only possible entry into the room behind the words. In so doing, the argument goes, we tend to sympathize to some extent with the speaker through whose words we must infer the situation. It is true, of course, that the speaker's words are all we have, but I think it unlikely that sym-

[1] New York, 1957, *passim*.

pathy is at all an adequate word for our relation to, say, Browning's
Duke. We may be fascinated by the size of his ego, by his gross
materialism, by his utter coldness; but our whole tendency is, I
think, to struggle out of his perspective into some other. It is this
tension between encasement in the form and our desire to escape
to a position of vantage which strikes us so intensely. It is this
tension which drives us to fill out the scene, objectify the Duke *and*
the envoy as if they were on a stage, analyze objectively the possible
ways that the Duke's words may be taken.

The same thing is true even in what we may call "inner" monologues, where the speaker is not actually talking to anyone but
speaking under his breath, as in Browning's "Soliloquy of the
Spanish Cloister" (not really a soliloquy), or where he is thinking,
as in Eliot's "The Love Song of J. Alfred Prufrock." There are
times, of course, when we are convinced that the speaker of "The
Spanish Cloister" may have a point. Brother Lawrence *is* probably
dull. But as the poem proceeds, any sympathy we might have had
for the speaker is countered by the revelation of his hypocrisy:

> G-r-r — there go, my heart's abhorrence!
>   Water your damned flower-pots, do!
> If hate killed men, Brother Lawrence,
>   God's blood, would not mine kill you!
> What? Your myrtle-bush wants trimming?
>   Oh, that rose has prior claims —
> Needs its leaden vase filled brimming?
>   Hell dry you up with its flames!
>
> At the meal we sit together:
>   *Salve tibi!* I must hear
> Wise talk of the kind of weather,
>   Sort of season, time of year:
> *Not a plenteous cork-crop: scarcely*
>   *Dare we hope oak-galls, I doubt:*
> *What's the Latin name for "parsley"?*
>   What's the Greek name for Swine's Snout?
>
> Whew! We'll have our platter burnished,
>   Laid with care on our own shelf!

With a fire-new spoon we're furnished,
    And a goblet for ourself,
Rinsed like something sacrificial
    Ere 'tis fit to touch our chaps —
Marked with L. for our initial!
    (He-he! There his lily snaps!)

Saint, forsooth! While brown Dolores
    Squats outside the Convent bank
With Sanchicha, telling stories,
    Steeping tresses in the tank,
Blue-black, lustrous, thick like horsehairs,
    — Can't I see his dead eye glow,
Bright as 'twere a Barbary corsair's?
    (That is, if he'd let it show!)

When he finishes refection,
    Knife and fork he never lays
Cross-wise, to my recollection,
    As do I, in Jesu's praise.
I, the Trinity illustrate,
    Drinking watered orange-pulp —
In three sips the Arian frustrate;
    While he drains his at one gulp!

Oh, those melons! if he's able
    We're to have a feast; so nice!
One goes to the Abbot's table,
    All of us get each a slice.
How go on your flowers? None double?
    Not one fruit-sort can you spy?
Strange! — And I, too, at such trouble,
    Keep them close-nipped on the sly!

There's a great text in Galatians,
    Once you trip on it, entails
Twenty-nine distinct damnations,
    One sure, if another fails;
If I trip him just a-dying,
    Sure of heaven as sure can be,
Spin him round and send him flying
    Off to Hell, a Manichee?

Or, my scrofulous French novel
    On grey paper with blunt type!

Simply glance at it, you grovel
   Hand and foot in Belial's gripe:
If I double back its pages
   At the woeful sixteenth print,
When he gathers his greengages,
   Ope a sieve and slip it in't?

Or, there's Satan! — one might venture
   Pledge one's soul to him, yet leave
Such a flaw in the indenture
   As he'd miss'till, past retrieve,
Blasted lay that rose-acacia
   We're so proud of! *Hy, Zy, Hine* . . .
'St, there's Vespers! *Plena gratiâ,*
Ave, Virgo! Gr-r-r — you swine!

Although we learn a good bit about Brother Lawrence and the life
of the monastery, what we really learn about is the speaker himself through the inconsistency of his position. Brother Lawrence
is revealed to be a bore whose interests are limited almost completely to his garden; possibly he is lecherous; but evidently, if he
is, he represses his feelings. Some of his actions may possibly be
interpreted as fawning upon the Abbot. But these failings are
nothing compared to those of the speaker, who is capable of vicious
resentment. The speaker makes too much display of piety in the
petty formalism of crossing his knife and fork at table and sipping
in threes. It is certain from his reading and his awareness of the
women at the tank that he is lecherous. And his plotting to catch
up Brother Lawrence leagues him with the Devil. I have probably
described the poem as more solemn and grim than it really is, for
the speaker is, of course, quite witty in expressing his exasperation,
the result of the inevitable friction of monastic life. In any case his
moment of unspoken diatribe lifts his whole life up out of time
and convinces us that we have observed something of his essential
nature.

Almost every dramatic monologue reveals something that the
speaker does not really mean to reveal or does not even understand
about himself. To reveal himself is, of course, not the speaker's

aim. Tennyson's most famous monologue is "Ulysses." The scene
is Ithaca, to which Ulysses has returned from Troy. Now he has
grown old, and Tennyson makes allusion to the legend that Ulysses
set out on another journey, not to return. Ulysses' speech does not
in content reveal more than he thinks it does. He indicates his own
restlessness:

> It little profits that an idle king,
> By this still hearth, among these barren crags,
> Matched with an aged wife, I mete and dole
> Unequal laws unto a savage race. . . .

He "cannot rest from travel," but at the same time he is not the
strong man of old. There is something tired in the poem's cadences.
The rhythms are languorous, almost as if Ulysses were longing for
an eternal quiet. He reveals more of this desire than the *content* of
the words reveals. Speaking to his mariners as they are about to
sail, he concludes:

> The lights begin to twinkle from the rocks;
> The long day wanes; The slow moon climbs; the deep
> Moans round with many voices. Come, my friends,
> 'Tis not too late to seek a newer world.
> Push off, and sitting well in order smite
> The sounding furrows; for my purpose holds
> To sail beyond the sunset, and the baths
> Of all the western stars, until I die.
> It may be that the gulfs will wash us down;
> It may be we shall touch the Happy Isles,
> And see the great Achilles, whom we knew.
> Though much is taken, much abides; and though
> We are not now that strength which in old days
> Moved earth and heaven; that which we are, we are, —
> One equal temper of heroic hearts,
> Made weak by time and fate, but strong in will
> To strive, to seek, to find, and not to yield.

The Tennysonian message to fight the good fight struggles om-
inously with the whole tone of the poem, and much of the poem's
interest lies in that struggle, unresolved to the end.

III

The dramatic monologue is not merely a Victorian phenomenon.
We find it in the poets of our own century — in T. S. Eliot, Ezra
Pound, Robert Lowell, and others. Each has made his own approach to the form. Browning wrote often in blank verse. Pound
has written one dramatic monologue called "Sestina: Alteforte" in
the difficult sestina form. Eliot's earliest major poem, "The Love
Song of J. Alfred Prufrock," loosens its rhythm to suggest the ebb
and flow of thought, rather than speech. His famous poem "The
Waste Land" can be thought of as being composed of snatches of
monologues, overheard by a main speaker. Lowell's "The Mills
of the Kavanaughs" contains passages which objectively set the
scene, but for the most part it is the reverie of a single person.

In some of these monologues the author takes us farther inside
his speaker than does Browning. In fact, the speaker sometimes
does not speak at all, even under his breath. We enter the area of
thought and daydream, and are subjected to unconscious switches
of subject and image. These are, in other words, "interior monologues." Browning's monk would like to castigate Brother Lawrence out loud, but does so under his breath. Prufrock does not
want to say his speech out loud, in fact probably could not. It
would be too embarrassing, it is not really speech at all, and finally
he is sure no one would understand him if he unburdened his mind:

> Would it have been worth while,
> To have bitten off the matter with a smile,
> To have squeezed the universe into a ball
> To roll it toward some overwhelming question,
> To say: "I am Lazarus, come from the dead,
> Come back to tell you all, I shall tell you all" —
> If one, settling a pillow by her head,
>   Should say: "That is not what I meant at all.
>   That is not it, at all."

Eliot's speaker *thinks* his monologue, but he is not always rational
or fully conscious of its direction. Eliot's method is affiliated with

the stream-of-consciousness technique of the twentieth-century novel. Prufrock seems to be addressing at times a lady friend, at other times himself. His mind looks ahead to the party to which he must go, darts back to consider himself, and then interrupts itself with images that seem to arise as motifs from below consciousness:

> In the room the women come and go
> Talking of Michelangelo.

There are moments of muttering despair:

> I should have been a pair of ragged claws
> Scuttling across the floors of silent seas,

of extreme self-doubt, of self-consciousness. We listen in, not behind the arras, as in Browning, but inside the speaker's mind, where all pretense is absent and the speaker is helpless to hide anything from us. Even though Prufrock searches himself, his search is not objective, as in the soliloquy, and he reveals more of himself than he realizes. Among recent monologues Lowell's "The Mills of the Kavanaughs" plunges to similar levels of the mental life. But the most extreme examples of the interior monologue exist in the prose of writers like James Joyce, Virginia Woolf, and Dorothy Richardson. In Joyce's minute articulations of the various levels of his characters' inner lives, the novel too turns drama into character. The monologues of Joyce are part of a still larger form to which they contribute, while a dramatic monologue as a poem must be a complete object in itself, creating words which form the door into a roomful of possible inferences, creating a short passage of time which can stand for a whole human existence.

IV

If not all twentieth-century poets have written dramatic monologues, certainly most of them have been influenced to make their poems dramatic. The influence is twofold — from Browning through Pound and others for the dramatic monologue, and from the metaphysicals through Eliot and Yeats for that brand of drama we see in Donne and Marvell. Both of these tendencies are popular in an

age where the poet recedes from his poem into the role of efficient
cause of his poem. The dramatic situation is objectified for purposes of irony, for example, in Eliot's "Sweeney" poems. The poet
comments, but with complete detachment. In poems where the
poet enters as an "I," we are usually invited to think of the "I" as a
fictional creation even though we may be asked to sympathize with
him. The speaker often informs us as if the action is going on *now,*
as in Karl Shapiro's "Auto Wreck." Such a poem puts things on a
stage, and we move through an action complete with denouement.
The poem is an imitation of a drama:

> Its quick soft silver bell beating, beating,
> And down the dark one ruby flare
> Pulsing out red light like an artery,
> The ambulance at top speed floating down
> Past beacons and illuminated clocks
> Wings in a heavy curve, dips down,
> And brakes speed, entering the crowd.
>
> The doors leap open, emptying light;
> Stretchers are laid out, the mangled lifted
> And stowed into the little hospital.
> Then the bell, breaking the hush, tolls once,
> And the ambulance with its terrible cargo
> Rocking, slightly rocking, moves away,
> As the doors, an afterthought, are closed.
>
> We are deranged, walking among the cops
> Who sweep glass and are large and composed.
> One is still making notes under a light.
> One with a bucket douches ponds of blood
> Into the street and gutter.
> One hangs lanterns on the wrecks that cling,
> Empty husks of locusts, to iron poles.
>
> Our throats were tight as tourniquets,
> Our feet were bound with splints, but now
> Like convalescents intimate and gauche,
> We speak through sickly smiles and warn
> With the stubborn saw of common sense,
> The grim joke and the banal resolution.
> The traffic moves around with care,

> But we remain, touching a wound
> That opens to our richest horror.
>
> Already old, the question Who shall die?
> Becomes unspoken Who is innocent?
> For death in war is done by hands;
> Suicide has cause and stillbirth, logic;
> And cancer, simple as a flower, blooms.
> But this invites the occult mind,
> Cancels our physics with a sneer,
> And spatters all we knew of denouement
> Across the expedient and wicked stones.

Although this poem begins with emphasis upon an exterior scene, it ends as an *inner* drama. The images of exterior action, the physical imagery of beating, hearts, veins, pulses, and blood, are brought "inside" to describe the mental reactions of those who have observed the wreck. The observers become the convalescents, "intimate and gauche." It is they who must ponder upon the meaning of the experience and suffer and convalesce from a "mental" injury parallel to the physical injuries they have observed.

W. B. Yeats' poem "The Mother of God," a series of questions asked by the Virgin Mary about the miracle of the Annunciation, is clearly an adaptation of the dramatic monologue. And many of his meditative poems have not escaped the influence of the form. In Yeats' beautiful poem "The Wild Swans at Coole" the speaker places himself within a scene very delicately described. He is observing a flock of swans. Suddenly the poem turns inward to memories of his first encounter with them, and it concludes with the poet's questioning the meaning of his experience. There is no answer to the questions he asks; drama is emphasized at the expense of easy solutions to the problem of time and change:

> The trees are in their autumn beauty,
> The woodland paths are dry,
> Under the October twilight the water
> Mirrors a still sky;
> Upon the brimming water among the stones
> Are nine-and-fifty swans.

The nineteenth autumn has come upon me
Since I first made my count;
I saw, before I had well finished,
All suddenly mount
And scatter wheeling in great broken rings
Upon their clamorous wings.

I have looked upon those brilliant creatures,
And now my heart is sore.
All's changed since I, hearing at twilight,
The first time on this shore,
The bell-beat of their wings above my head,
Trod with a lighter tread.

Unwearied still, lover by lover,
They paddle in the cold
Companionable streams or climb the air;
Their hearts have not grown old;
Passion or conquest, wander where they will,
Attend upon them still.

But now they drift on the still water,
Mysterious, beautiful;
Among what rushes will they build,
By what lake's edge or pool
Delight men's eyes when I awake some day
To find they have flown away?

Yeats' poem is meditative as well as dramatic. It might well be called an ode. But the careful observation of the scene, the remembrance filtered through the speaker's mind, and the final questioning call attention to the dramatic structure holding and giving shape to the meditation. The speaker is a player in a drama of observation.

Yeats may also violently thrust a scene upon us, as in "Leda and the Swan," where the sonnet form contains drama. It is as if a curtain had suddenly risen. Then the poem may turn inward, as in "The Cold Heaven":

Suddenly I saw the cold and rook-delighting heaven
That seemed as though ice burned and was but the more ice,
And thereupon imagination and the heart were driven
So wild that every casual thought of that and this

5   Vanished, and left but memories, that should be out of season
      With the hot blood of youth, of love crossed long ago;
      And I took all the blame out of all sense and reason,
      Until I cried and trembled and rocked to and fro,
      Riddled with light. Ah! when the ghost begins to quicken,
10   Confusion of the death-bed over, is it sent
      Out naked on the roads, as the books say, and stricken
      By the injustice of the skies for punishment?

Here the poet speaks not in the present tense, as in "The Wild Swans at Coole," but in a past brought virtually into the present by the abrupt beginning. Two dramas are going on at once: first, the past experience described in the first eight and a half lines; second, the speaker's dwelling now upon that experience and struggling to find its significance. That he really does not discover the meaning is no blot upon the poem, but simply a continuation of the drama.

As we read through Yeats' poetry we find the poet repeatedly recreating the past dramatically or speaking directly out of a present situation, as if he had the main role in a play, the scene of which is the whole world:

(1) What shall I do with this absurdity —

(2) That is no country for old men. . . .

(3) I climb to the tower-top and lean upon broken stone

(4) I walk through the long schoolroom questioning

(5) Around me the images of thirty years.

(6) Midnight has come, and the great Christ Church Bell
And many a lesser bell sound through the room.

(7) The unpurged images of day recede.

These seven passages are beginnings of some of the best poems by Yeats. The first two are direct statement, as if the speaker were soliloquizing; we are invited to imagine him thinking. The third, fourth, and fifth set scenes; they are virtually stage directions before the poem turns inward to the speaker's thoughts. The last two are a little more subjective: they set both scene *and* mood. These dramatic beginnings are characteristic of Yeats' and of much modern poetry.

When we look at "The Wild Swans at Coole" and "The Cold Heaven," we notice the poet is not committed to metrical verse patterns but rather to accentual arrangement. The effort appears to be to make the lyric natural and even a bit loose in order to suggest the spontaneous overflow of the speaker's feelings. But the speaker is objectified as a dramatic character. One suspects that experimentation in versification may be intrinsic to the dramatic character of a poem. This can be seen in our century not only in Yeats' interesting rhythms but also in the work of such poets as Ezra Pound and William Carlos Williams. Among some poets the cadence of the spoken phrase replaces the foot, the syllable, or the counted accents as the dominant rhythmical unit. Fairly early in his career we find Pound objecting to composition according to metronomic beat and holding to something analogous to the musical phrase. Williams has remarked that there is really no such thing as free verse. Verse has rhythm, even if it is not metrical, syllabic, quantitative, etc. Amy Lowell adopted "strophe" as a word characteristic of the free verse rhythmic unit. Oddly enough, after borrowing this term from Greek drama, Miss Lowell's free verse movement, combining with "imagism," died from an utter dependence upon the static image that caused a consequent lack of dramatic action. Poetry attaches itself to drama in a variety of ways, seeks constantly to contain drama or become a part of it. In the twentieth century this tendency toward drama and the dramatic can be seen in the works of Eliot and Yeats, two distinguished verse dramatists who have employed the dramatic in their poems.

Some Suggested Reading

Honan, Park, *Browning's Characters.*
Langbaum, Robert, *The Poetry of Experience.*

8 Symbolist Lyric:

THE INNER EDGE OF POETRY

Meaning and context. Romantic distinctions between allegory and symbolism. Theological and metaphysical sources. Psychological aspects: the dream world: Freud and Jung. Suggestion: Baudelaire, Mallarmé. The untranslatable symbol: self-containment of meaning. Blake's allegory and symbolism. Yeats' swans. Relation to the dramatic monologue and metaphysical poem.

1

We know that the meaning of any word or pharse depends partially upon its context. The word "oh," for instance, can be uttered so as to have opposite meanings depending upon the speaker's tone and upon the social context in which the tone is employed. Not only are meanings established by context; similarly, they are also limited and eliminated according to contextural use. Taken in context, the apparently simple statement, "He's a fine fellow," can be made to mean not only the opposite of what the words in isolation suggest, but any number of other things as well. All language has this potentiality, though in some situations writers try to purge their statements of all but direct and apparent meaning. Poetic language depends to a tremendous degree upon its construction, its total form. The parts of a poem have complete meaning in relation to the whole. Lewis Carroll's supposedly nonsensical poem "Jabberwocky" illustrates the point. Take the words "brillig," "wabe," and "toves" out of context and they lose their

163

context helps us to sense what overtones each
meant to carry:

illig, and the slithy toves
gyre and gimble in the wabe;
msy were the borogoves,
d the mome raths outgrabe.

Alice's Humpty Dumpty interprets these words with considerable
freedom, and we are free, I think, to disagree. It is not difficult to
notice obvious suggestions, some noted by Carroll himself: "slithy,"
for example, suggests "sly," "lithe," "slimy," "slither"; and the other
words send forth their own auras of meaning. But the suggestiveness of this word is primarily created by its context, the whole statement inviting us to invent meanings which will fit into it. We
would not waste our time with these inventions if we confronted
the nonsense words in isolation from each other. It is noticeable
also that the whole poem "Jabberwocky" is more meaningful in
the context of the book *Through the Looking-Glass*, to which it
belongs, than when it is taken alone. Meaning is involved with
context: word in phrase and sentence, sentence in stanza and
poem, poem in literature as a total form.

Each of these units is a symbol, dependent upon its context. Let
us take first the word as a unit within a poem. Beginning with the
romantic movement, poets and critics made a distinction between
"symbolism" and "allegory." It was essentially, as Northrop Frye
has observed, a contrast between "a 'concrete' approach to symbols
which begins with images of actual things and works outward to
ideas and propositions, and an 'abstract' approach which begins
with the idea and then tries to find a concrete image to represent
it." [1] Among the romantic poets a little more than this is actually
involved. Coleridge, for example, is obviously influenced by theology and metaphysics:

Now an allegory is but a translation of abstract notions into a
picture-language, which is itself nothing but an abstraction from

[1] *Anatomy of Criticism*, p. 89.

objects of the senses; the principal being more worthless even than its phantom proxy, both alike unsubstantial, and the former shapeless to boot. On the other hand a symbol . . . is characterized by a translucence of the special in the individual, or of the general in the special, or of the universal in the general; above all by the translucence of the eternal through and in the temporal.[2]

For Coleridge and several other romantic poets, allegory is a substitution of one known object for an abstract concept. Most eighteenth-century personification, eschewed by Wordsworth, can easily slide over to allegory. It is not a long step from a personification such as "bravery retired to his den" to an allegory in which, say, a lion represents bravery.

Coleridge finds symbolism working in the opposite direction, seeking the universal in the particular, as Goethe asserted. The symbol begins with a particular in order to express something apparently inexpressible in any other way. It does not seek to express a concept particularly, for no concept lurks behind the symbol so defined. Behind it, the romantic theorist most often said, was the eternal or ineffable. It is clear that in bringing the infinite (precisely what many twentieth-century critics dislike about romantic poetry) into his definition, Coleridge was strongly influenced by theology. A modern theologian, Edwyn Bevan, discusses symbols in a theological context; his commentary is suggestive of the romantic attitude:

A symbol . . . means something presented to the senses or the imagination — usually to the senses — which stands for something else. Symbolism in that way runs through the whole of life. . . . But we have, for our purposes, to make a distinction at the outset between two different kinds of symbols. [The first of these kinds is even more mechanical than the romantic poet's "allegory."] There are visible objects or sounds which stand for something of which we already have direct knowledge. Such symbols are not intended to give us any information about the nature of the thing or things symbolized, but to remind us of them, or tell us something about their action at the particular moment, or prompt us to act in a certain way at the particular moment

[2] "The Statesman's Manual" (1816), *Complete Works* (W. G. T. Shedd, ed.), New York, 1884, I, pp. 437–438.

because of them [the Union Jack, the sound of a trumpet, etc.]. . . . The other kind of symbols purport to give information about the things they symbolize, to convey knowledge of their nature. . . . But also in religion things are presented to the senses, or ideas presented to the mind, which purport, not to call to the mind other things within the experience of the worshipper, but to convey to him knowledge of things beyond the range of any human experience.[3]

In other words, the most profound religious symbols have behind them something we cannot experience directly or conceive of adequately in discursive language. Now we can understand what C. S. Lewis means in *The Allegory of Love* when, following the romantic distinction, he argues that allegory is a mode of expression but symbolism is a mode of thought. Allegory thus defined is verbal substitution, while symbolism is a method of making things known. The romantic critics applied their definitions rather rigidly, and symbolism was at once associated with mystical experience. In Carlyle's *Sartor Resartus*, it is described as follows:

In the Symbol proper, what we can call a Symbol, there is ever, more or less distinctly and directly, some embodiment and revelation of the Infinite; the Infinite is made to blend itself with the Finite, to stand visible, and as it were, attainable there. By Symbols, accordingly, is man guided and commanded, made happy, made wretched. He everywhere finds himself encompassed with Symbols, recognized as such or not recognized: the Universe is but one vast symbol of God; nay if thou wilt have it, what is Man himself but a Symbol of God. . . . Not a Hut he builds but is the visible embodiment of a Thought; but bears visible record of invisible things; but is, in the transcendental sense, symbolical as well as real.[4]

The idea of the symbol as a mode of revelation extends into the later nineteenth century, even into our own time. In his study of Blake, published in 1893, W. B. Yeats held to the idea of the symbol as a mystical expression. He went farther than Carlyle in showing how it actually functions in a poem:

[3] *Symbolism and Belief*, Boston, 1957, pp. 11–14.
[4] *Sartor Resartus* (1833–1834), New York, 1921, pp. 195–196.

> A perfect mystical symbol or fable can be read in any region of
> nature and thought — mineral, meteoric, religious, philosophical
> — it is all one. Things we have to give in *succession* in our explan-
> atory prose are set forth *simultaneously* in Blake's verse.[5]

Here Yeats accepts Blake's idea that allegory often contains some
"vision" (a term in Blake roughly equivalent to "symbolism"),
that is, has some translatable meaning but often contains beyond
that meaning significance expressible only in its own terms. Yeats
also allows for what we have called elsewhere "ambiguity" — the
coexistence of different relevant meanings in the same symbol. But
symbolist theory is generally more radical than Yeats' statement
indicates. It holds that what the symbol says can *never* be set forth
in succession.

II

If symbolist theory begins in association with theology and a striving to represent the infinite and eternal, it does not necessarily end
that way. It has two other important aspects. The first is the psychological. Coleridge, typically romantic, saw art as the inner
made outer through the use of symbols to express the mind. Thus
a symbol, in another aspect, is not a representation of the infinite
and eternal but of the inner and mental. This idea is suggested also
by Charles Baudelaire (1821–1867), the great French poet, who
in revolt against naturalistic art, raises the question of whether
external nature really exists at all:

> In recent years we have heard it said in a thousand different ways,
> "Copy nature; only copy nature. There is no greater delight, no
> finer triumph than an excellent copy of nature." And this doctrine
> (the enemy of art) was alleged to apply not only to painting but
> to all the arts, even to the novel and to poetry. . . . A man of
> imagination would certainly have had the right to reply: "I con-
> sider it useless and tedious to represent what *exists*, because noth-
> ing that *exists* satisfies me. Nature is ugly, and I prefer the mon-
> sters of my fancy to what is positively trivial." And yet it would

[5] *The Works of William Blake* (E. J. Ellis and W. B. Yeats, ed.), London,
1893, I, p. 287.

have been even more philosophical to ask the doctrinaires in question first of all whether they were quite certain of the existence of
external nature. . . .[6]

Though Baudelaire's poetry explores the mental world, his theory
of symbolism also included, in his doctrine of "correspondences,"
a mystique. The human imagination must *put together,* so to
speak, the parts of the universe, which seem diverse and unrelated:
"The whole visible universe is but a storehouse of images and signs
to which the imagination will give a relative place and value; it is
a sort of pasture which the imagination must digest and trans-
form." There are psychological relations between colors, sounds,
etc., which are really more than psychological; for the world of
imaginative relations is, as Baudelaire saw it, the real world, the
only reality:

> Nature is a temple of living pillars
> Where often words emerge, confused and dim;
> and man goes through this forest, with familiar
> eyes of symbols always watching him.
>
> Like prolonged echoes mingling far away
> in a unity tenebrous and profound,
> vast as the night and as the limpid day,
> perfumes, sounds, and colors correspond.
>
> There are perfumes as cool as children's flesh,
> sweet as oboes, as meadows green and fresh;
> — others, triumphant and corrupt and rich,
>
> with power to fill the infinite expanses,
> like amber, incense, musk, and benzoin, which
> sing the transports of the soul and senses.

This sonnet, the famous "Correspondences," is concerned with the
convergence of sensations and the objects which evoke them, the
inner and outer worlds, but also the relations between sensations
and between objects. The poem "suggests" more than it says. Its
images reflect the attitude of the later French poet, Stéphane
Mallarmé (1842–1898):

[6] "The Queen of the Faculties," *The Mirror of Art* (J. Mayne, trans. & ed.),
Garden City, 1956, pp. 233–234.

I feel that the young poets are nearer than the Parnassians to the poetic ideal. The latter still treat their subjects as the old philosophers and orators did: that is, they present things directly, whereas I think that they should be presented allusively. Poetry lies in the *contemplation* of things, in the image emanating from the reveries which things arouse in us. The Parnassians take something in its entirety and simply exhibit it; in so doing, they fall short of mystery; they fail to give our minds that exquisite joy which consists of believing that we are creating something. To *name* an object is largely to destroy poetic enjoyment, which comes from gradual divination. The ideal is to *suggest* the object. It is the perfect use of this mystery which constitutes symbol.[7]

This passage may give the impression, as Mallarmé's own poems often do, of advocating willful obscurity, purposeful concealment of what might have been expressed in another way. But although Mallarmé represents an extreme view, his theory holds that the poetic statement is an effort to get at experience that cannot be expressed otherwise. By "mystery" he does not, then, mean obfuscation.

Baudelaire's obviously psychological interest and that of the English romantic poets, especially Blake, suggest that symbolist poetry has an intimate relation to modern psychology, particularly the theories of Sigmund Freud and Carl Jung. Actually, however, in spite of its psychological interest symbolist theory is at odds with Freud's conception of the symbol. From the symbolist point of view Freud is an allegorical interpreter. Freud saw the dream symbol as a concrete representation of an idea inaccessible because the mind distorts the real dream into a "manifest dream." We know only the manifest dream at first hand and must interpret it in order to arrive at its latent repressed content. In Freud's sense the symbol is a curious translation of something ultimately explainable but also repressible and inaccessible except through the interpretation, which can be adequate as a statement of its meaning. It is clear that Freud's conception is nearer to romantic "allegory" than to symbolism. A Freudian interpreter of literature is strictly an

---

[7] "The Evolution of Literature," *Selected Prose, Poems, Essays, and Letters* (Bradford Cook, trans. & ed.), Baltimore, 1956, p. 21.

allegorical interpreter (he tries to state exactly what the symbols mean according to psychoanalytical methods). A poet who self-consciously employs so-called Freudian symbols is a modern allegorist, though his poem may include and transcend allegorical meanings.

Jung's conception of the dream image differs from Freud's. He sees the dream as a concrete representation of an idea that cannot find any other possible expression. The dream symbol is therefore like the poetic symbol. Jung's "archetypes," or what we may prefer to call traditional symbols, stand for psychic experience beyond the boundaries of conceptual thought:

> From the very first beginnings of human society onward man's efforts to give his vague intimations a binding form have left their traces. Even in the Rhodesian cliff-drawings of the Old Stone Age there appears, side by side with the most amazingly life-like representations of animals, an abstract pattern — a double cross contained in a circle. This design has turned up in every cultural region, more or less, and we find it today not only in Christian churches but in Tibetan monasteries as well. It is the so-called sun wheel, and as it dates from a time when no one had thought of wheels as a mechanical device, it cannot have had its source in any experience of the external world. It is rather a symbol that stands for a psychic happening; it covers an experience of the inner world.[8]

Jung suggests that every poet must employ mythology "to give his experience its most fitting expression. . . . The primordial experience is the source of his creativeness; it cannot be fathomed, and therefore requires mythological imagery to give it form. In itself it offers no words or images, for it is a vision seen 'as in a glass darkly.' It is merely a deep presentiment that strives to find expression." Jung's attitude toward symbolism returns to that of his German romantic forebears. The interesting point is that his analysis of the symbol provides a link between psychology and literary symbolism, while Freud's provides a link between psychology and allegorical interpretation. Freud has, of course, greatly influenced

[8] "Psychology and Literature," *Modern Man in Search of a Soul* (1933), New York, n.d., pp. 163–164.

modern writers to use dream imagery, and he has influenced critics to interpret this writing as Freudian allegory. Critics have gone on to interpret all literature in Freudian terms, and it is here that their interpretations are often dubious, for they tend to shut off the broad, expansive significance of the symbol in favor of a limited allegorical translation.

III

The second aspect of symbolist theory is the idea of the symbol containing its own meaning. In this aspect the symbol does not necessarily stand for the infinite and eternal, a meaning distorted by the dream censor, or definable psychic experience. In this aspect the poem is *itself*. Its meaning lies not in what it or its parts point to but in the relations among its parts. Perhaps the analogy of mathematics is helpful here. In mathematics the symbol does not stand for something beyond itself. Mathematical symbols have no denotation. They *mean* in relation to each other. True, they can be given values that point toward the outer world, and these values can be absorbed by their total form; but basically their meaning is contextual. Frye has observed:

> In all literary verbal structures the final direction of meaning is inward. In literature the standards of outward meaning are secondary, for literary works do not pretend to describe or assert, and hence are not true, not false, and yet not tautological either.[9]

It is clear that Mallarmé's poems represent an extremist view in the same camp, the difference being that Mallarmé attempts to eliminate even the secondary outward direction of his poem in favor of absolute inwardness. This resentment against denotation, which Mallarmé associates with scientific materialism and literary naturalism, leads him in his famous sonnet *"Ses purs ongles . . ."* even to coining the word "ptyx," which, having no dictionary meaning, *must* gain all its significance from its context.

[9] *Anatomy of Criticism*, in the third essay.

Her pure nails very high dedicating their onyx,
Anguish, this midnight, supports a torch where burns
many a vesperal dream consumed by the Phoenix
which is not collected in the cinereal urn

on the credenzas, in the bare room: no ptyx,
abolished bibelot empty and sonorous
(for the Master has gone to draw tears from the Styx
with the sole object by which the Nothing is honored).

But near the window open on the north
a gold is dying perhaps in the decor
of unicorns kicking fire at a nixie,

who, defunct and nude in the mirror, as yet
in the oblivion bound by the frame, is fixed
of scintillations forthwith the septet.[10]

Few poets go so far as Mallarmé does here in rejecting outward
meaning. Nevertheless, there has been a constant barrage of statements from modern poets about the independence of poetry from
naïve denotation of objects and ideas. The same idea occurs in late-
nineteenth-century assertions that all art aspires to the condition of
music, in many tenets of so-called "art for art's sake." In recent
years there is Archibald MacLeish's "Ars Poetica," which is a symbolist version of the verse essay:

A poem should be palpable and mute
As a globed fruit

Dumb
As old medallions to the thumb

Silent as the sleeve-worn stone
Of casement ledges where the moss has grown —
A poem should be wordless
As the flight of birds

            .   .   .   .   .   .

[10] For a brief, helpful analysis of this poem see the notes by its translator,
C. F. MacIntyre, in *Stéphane Mallarmé: Selected Poems*, Berkeley and Los
Angeles, 1957, pp. 147–148.

> A poem should not mean
> But be.

Here is Marianne Moore's similar statement in "Poetry":

> nor till the poets among us can be
> "literalists of
> the imagination" — above
> insolence and triviality and can present
>
> for inspection, imaginary gardens with real toads in
> them, shall we have
> it.

The phrase "literalist of the imagination" is one used by Yeats to describe Blake. Yeats himself made one of the most interesting assertions of this sort in his curious prose work *A Vision*, in which he develops a system of symbolism based upon astrology and occultism:

> Now that the system stands out clearly in my imagination I regard [the symbols] as stylistic arrangements of experience comparable to the cubes in the drawings of Wyndham Lewis and to the ovoids in the sculpture of Brancusi. They have helped me to hold in a single thought reality and justice.[11]

Thus Yeats asserts the inner integrity of the major symbols of his book and invites us to gather the whole work up into our minds as a unit. To this kind of idea we shall return in Chapter 9.

IV

Yeats called Blake "the first writer of modern times to preach the indissoluble marriage of all great art with symbol." [12] It is well to look at one of Blake's poems to discover what peculiar quality moved Yeats to make that statement.

> O Rose, thou art sick!
> The invisible worm

[11] *A Vision* (1938), New York, 1956, p. 25.
[12] "William Blake and His Illustrations," *Essays and Introductions*, London, 1961, p. 116.

That flies in the night,
In the howling storm,

Has found out thy bed
Of crimson joy:
And his dark secret love
Does thy life destroy.

("The Sick Rose")

This poem has been examined recently in at least three different textbook discussions of symbolism; all three are reluctant in varying degrees to commit themselves to a specific interpretation.[13] After several tentative remarks Drew concludes, "This suggests some evil devouring sexuality that destroys instead of creating, bringing mortal sickness to the crimson joy." Abrams interprets in very general terms: "Blake's worm-eaten rose symbolizes such matters as the destruction wrought by furtiveness, deceit, and hypocrisy in what should be a frank and joyous relation of physical love." Both of these statements are helpful, but neither is, as the authors affirm, complete. Both are reluctant to commit themselves to single readings. Both hold that the poem's meaning is ultimately itself and that a full interpretation would be infinite in length.

We must conclude that in the terms we have set up all interpretation is allegorizing unless it limits itself to pointing out relations among the elements of the poem. We see also that Mallarmé, with his coined word "ptyx," made allegorical interpretation, at least of that word, impossible. It exists almost totally in relation to the poem's other elements.

Yet in spite of all this it is possible that a "symbolist" poem can *contain* allegory, just as according to Blake allegory can contain some vision. We know that some of Blake's long poems contain allegories of contemporary history and personal experience intermixed with complex undefinable symbols. "The Sick Rose" invites a certain amount of allegorical reading. By this I mean that an

[13] They are M. H. Abrams, *A Glossary of Literary Terms*, New York, 1957, pp. 95–96; Elizabeth Drew, *Poetry: A Modern Guide to Its Understanding and Enjoyment*, New York, 1959, pp. 63–64; and M. K. Danziger and W. S. Johnson, *An Introduction to Literary Criticism*, Boston, 1961, pp. 30–31.

allegorical reading does not have to be simply a cautious step in an endless groping toward the poem's meaning. It may instead reveal a very definite isolable meaning within the larger symbolic totality. Our third interpretation, as expressed by Danziger and Johnson, asserts, "It would be very dubious, in this instance, to insist upon the flower's being a woman, and much too far-fetched to suppose that the poem has to do specifically with a loss of virginity." Perhaps what they say here is true, but with slight variations we might have something accurate and acceptable: The flower is feminine, the worm masculine sexuality, and the poem is about a seduction in a "bed" of nature and of love. I do not see how this can be denied, particularly in the light of Freudian allegorization in our own time and the obvious use of sexual allegory of this sort throughout Blake's works. Our mistake would be to stop here, for the simple allegorical equation merely sets the symbolist aspects of the poem in motion. In that area we can only indicate *directions* of significance. Nor will this poem be adequately understood until its tone is considered and the attitude of the speaker in his own drama is taken into account. Finally it must be remembered that a rose *is* a rose.

It is quite possible that the poet often sees as allegorical what his contemporary reader sees as symbolic or hopelessly obscure. A reason for this might be that the poet is in advance of his contemporaries. I suspect that the allegorical aspects of his poems were clear enough to Blake; although it took a century of psychological study of dreams to reveal the mode of allegorical statement being used. It may be the same in our relation to some contemporary poets. But it is also true that in a good poem there is a symbolical aspect which we can never adequately allegorize away, no matter how much progress is made in psychology or the other sciences.

V

In the first year of our century, one of its greatest poets, Yeats, published an essay called "The Symbolism of Poetry" in praise of

Arthur Symons' study of the French symbolist poets.[14] His remarks begin with a quotation from Symons himself, who wrote, "Symbolism, as seen in the writers of our day, would have no value if it were not seen also, under one disguise or another, in every great imaginative writer." This is a fair statement of the case. Later in his essay Yeats remarks that poetry "must have the perfection that escapes analysis, the subtleties that have a new meaning every day." His point is that you can state your likes and dislikes, describe, or analyze with words not always carefully chosen; but in order to "give a body" to something, your words must be "subtle, complex, full of mysterious life." Yeats was moving toward a distinction between the language of logical analysis and that of poetry. His attitudes were partly the result of his rejection of naturalistic writing:

> The scientific movement brought with it a literature, which was always tending to lose itself in externalities of all kinds, in opinion, in declamation, in picturesque writing, in word-painting, or in what Mr. Symons has called an attempt "to build in brick and mortar inside the covers of a book"; and now writers have begun to dwell upon the element of evocation; of suggestion, upon what we call the symbolism in great writers.

Every great poem, for Yeats, has an element beyond interpretation. His own lyric "The Wild Swans at Coole" (quoted in Chapter 7) might be a test case. Surely it is neither erudite nor obscure. Descriptive of an apparently simple experience, the poem evades interpretation. In his book on Yeats, Donald Stauffer devotes considerable space to a discussion of this poem and the use of swans throughout Yeats' poetry. Nowhere are Yeats' swans fully explained, although in a letter Yeats himself wrote that the swan in one of his poems was "a symbol of inspiration, I think." Even that interpretation is so general and so clearly qualified by "I think" that we cannot accept it as final. In another poem he wrote:

> Some moralist or mythological poet
> Compares the solitary soul to a swan;

[14] "The Symbolism of Poetry" (1900), *Essays and Introductions*, pp. 153–164.

I am satisfied with that,
Satisfied if a troubled mirror show it,
Before that brief gleam of its life be gone,
An image of its state;
The wings half spread for flight,
The breast thrust out in pride
Whether to play, or to ride
Those winds that clamour of approaching night.

("Nineteen Hundred and Nineteen")

Even here the statement is not meant to define the swan's meaning fully. It is part of a dramatic utterance. Nevertheless, it is applicable to "The Wild Swans at Coole" in a tentative sort of way. As an interpretation it merely provides a direction into the symbol. In that poem the swans, like Keats' nightingale, survive in time, unchanging like the soul to which Yeats refers above. They are also images of inspiration. Their intimacy with the whole of abiding nature is indicated by the context: the imagery of treading and metronomic beating which suggests the passing away of things much as does the tolling of "forlorn" in Keats' ode. The swans are beautiful, delightful, passionate, riding smoothly on the "cold, companionable" flux of water. But they elude all of these formulations, just as their essential being eludes the speaker of the poem.

In his essay on symbolism Yeats displays two lines by Robert Burns as examples of what he calls emotional symbols:

The white moon is setting behind the white wave,
And Time is setting with me, O!

and he remarks:

Take from them the whiteness of the moon and of the wave, whose relation to the setting of Time is too subtle for the intellect, and you take from them their beauty. But, when all are together, moon and wave and whiteness and setting Time and the last melancholy cry, they evoke an emotion which cannot be evoked by any other arrangement of colours and sounds and forms.

The evocation, then, is the whole poetic statement. Outside a poem Yeats' swans are merely swans, Rilke's panther merely a

panther, Blake's tiger merely a tiger, Hart Crane's bridge merely
a span between Brooklyn and Manhattan. But in their poems, in
literature, they evolve a meaning never fully contained by explication.

Poems gain intensity and concentration of meaning by belong-
ing to literature as a total form. Blake's rose is not exactly the
symbolical rose of paradise which Dante describes in the *Paradiso*;
but its meaning has some relation to it. Even the bells "ringing
with rose" in Cummings' "Impression" are related, however, tenu-
ously, to the same literary cluster. Nor is the relation always that
of one poet's influence upon another. It is instead a matter of the
nature and the potentialities and the limitations of literature.
When T. S. Eliot observed that immature poets copy and ma-
ture ones steal, he was talking about matters of this sort. The elements of literature are images embodied in poems, stories, and
myths. Gérard de Nerval wrote, "I then saw vaguely drifting into
form, plastic images of antiquity, which outlined themselves, became definite, and seemed to represent symbols of which I only
sensed the idea with difficulty." Most of Nerval's poems seem to be
descriptions of such experiences, one of the most direct of which
is the following:

> There is a tune for which I would give all
> Rossini, all of Weber and Mozart,
> an old tune, languid and funereal,
> that charms me only with its secret art.
>
> Now every time I happen to hear it sung,
> my soul grows younger by two centuries:
> it's the reign of Louis Treize . . . and I think I see
> a green hill yellowed by the setting sun;
>
> Then an old brick château with stone corners,
> and the leaded glass of the windows, color of rose,
> begirt by great parks, where a river flows,
> bathing the stones as it glides among the flowers;
>
> then a lady, at the tall window of her chamber,
> a blonde with dark eyes, in an old-time gown . . .

> whom I have seen before, perhaps, and known
> in another existence — and whom I remember!
>
> ("Fantasy")

Not all symbolical poems need be so mysterious. Nerval exploits this aspect of poetic meaning, but all true poems have it to some degree and cannot be "solved" by analysis. Since this is foreign to the main direction of our education, we are sometimes impatient to the point of dismissing the poet's statement as too ephemeral or "unrealistic." Perhaps it is our own faith in logic and analysis which we should re-examine in order to see whether *it* is logical enough. For what is a logic that limits the reality of which Shakespeare, Dante, Milton, and all the other great poets spoke?

VI

Before returning to some of these questions in a larger theoretical framework, I shall conclude this chapter with brief remarks about the popularity of the dramatic monologue and metaphysical style in an age of essentially symbolist poetry. The drama implies a completed world of created characters. Inquiries into such subjects as the girlhood of Shakespeare's heroines, while amusing, have nothing to do with the heroines themselves, for they have no existence except in the plays themselves. In this sense a play seems to illustrate the symbolist conception of aesthetic self-containment or inwardness very clearly. The dramatic monologue makes the same point. It is clearly, also, full of suggestion. In it the drama's passage of time is itself symbolic of the whole life and being of the speaker. We can never exhaust speculation about the Duke. It is not too much to say that the modern interest in the "dramatic" is a symbolist interest.

In the eyes of a good many critics symbolist poetry has effected a marriage with metaphysical style. Cleanth Brooks has suggested that in a poem like Yeats' "Sailing to Byzantium" we notice a metaphysical tendency to assimilate "diverse materials" and at the same time a symbolistic use of language opposed to scientific discourse. Brooks observes that in the subtlety of their description of feelings the metaphysicals and symbolists have much in common. Nevertheless, there are differences. Donne's compasses and Yeats' swans are different sorts of images. Donne's image is clipped and trimmed, limited in its expansiveness (though the poem as a whole is not). It is illustrative. Yeats' swans are expansive.

The inner edge of poetry is, therefore, the symbolic aspect of the poem. Past that edge the poem can become, rather than more expansive, irresponsible and obscure if the poet indulges in a totally private imagery given meaning neither by tradition and convention nor by form and context.

Some Suggested Reading

Baudelaire, Charles, "The Queen of the Faculties" in *The Mirror of Art*.

Hoffman, Frederick J., *Freudianism and the Literary Mind*.

Hough, Graham, *Image and Experience*.

Jung, C. G., *Modern Man in Search of a Soul*.

MacIntyre, C. F. (translator), *French Symbolist Poetry*.

Mallarmé, Stéphane, *Selected Prose Poems, Essays, and Letters* (Bradford Cook, editor and translator).

Symons, Arthur, *The Symbolist Movement in Literature*.

Tindall, W. Y., *The Literary Symbol*.

Yeats, W. B., "The Symbolism of Poetry," in *Ideas of Good and Evil*.

9 A Theory:

THE LITERARY COSMOS

The idea of multiple worlds: Kant and Cassirer. The language of the literary cosmos: Wheelwright. Literary space and time. Literary and dream worlds. Extremes of the literary cosmos are the extremes of man's imagination. Dominant themes. Patterns of paradox. Artist as Creator in Coleridge.

1

All respectable discussions of literature must have a philosophic basis. Sometimes the basis is left unmentioned; sometimes it is not well understood by the author. It is up to anyone talking about literature, or anything else, for that matter, to be aware of the assumptions underlying his remarks. It is preferable, I think, that he reveal his assumptions, however briefly. The purpose of this chapter, then, is to present in the very thinnest of outlines a position out of which the previous discussions have arisen. I hope that the chapter will suggest the importance of poetry in relation to other means of gaining knowledge, that it will on the one hand indicate comparisons between poetry and science and on the other relate the study of poetry to philosophy, where all study should begin and end. Nor should such a discussion limit itself to poetry, but should expand to encompass the other literary arts as well.

My first assumption is that all modes of knowing reality are really constructions or creations of reality — symbolic systems which the human mind has made. We can never know anything

181

beyond these systems, and they are to all practical intents and purposes our realities. We judge the truth or falsity of their propositions according to the inner structural laws of each system. The laws of scientific method were developed through a long period during which man struggled from primitivism to some degree of civilization, casting off superstitions or mythical explanations of natural phenomena, developing principles of induction and deduction, and then critiques of those principles. One of the attempts to isolate the categories of science (or, as he called them, of the understanding) was made by the philosopher Immanuel Kant (1724–1804) — quantity, quality, relation, and modality. Whether these are the proper or only categories of science need not detain us here. The point that must detain us is that the world which science constructs, the scientific cosmos, operates by laws which are inconceivable except within the containing form of categories of thought. There are, of course, a variety of systems within science itself, each with its own principles of judgment — as in the case of the various systems of geometry.

I would suggest, as the philosopher Ernst Cassirer did, that there are systems other than that of scientific method, which operate not within the categories of the understanding but within a set of parallel but contrasting categories. In his *Philosophy of Symbolic Forms*, as well as in the later *Essay on Man*, Cassirer distinguished a variety of these symbolic forms or systems — religion, art, mythical thought (a primitive form which must gradually disappear into the others), and science. His analyses of mythical thought and of science are fairly complete, as is his long and fascinating discussion of language. But his discussion of art, limited to the later *Essay on Man*, stops short of presenting to us the categories of art, in other words the form of the artistic cosmos. He does point the necessary direction, however. He writes:

> Like all the other symbolic forms art is not the mere reproduction of a ready-made, given reality. It is one of the ways leading to an objective view of things and of human life. . . . From a merely theoretical point of view we may subscribe to the words of Kant that mathematics is the "pride of human reason." But for this

triumph of scientific reason we have to pay a very high price. Science means abstraction, and abstraction is always an impoverishment of reality. The form of things as they are described in scientific concepts tends more and more to become mere formulae. These formulae are of a surprising simplicity. A single formula, like the Newtonian law of gravitation, seems to comprise and explain the whole structure of our material universe. It would seem as though reality were not only accessible to our scientific abstractions but exhaustible by them. But as soon as we approach the field of art this proves to be an illusion. For the aspects of things are innumerable, and they vary from one moment to another. Any attempt to comprehend them within a simple formula would be in vain.[1]

Cassirer proceeds to remark that all aesthetic schools should admit that "art is an independent 'universe of discourse.' " Of course, like science, art covers a very large field of endeavor, and there are deep and important differences among the arts, so that what we have are systems within systems — much like the various geometries — painting, music, sculpture, literature, etc.

We must not blame Cassirer for failing to map out the literary world for us. Beginning as a philosopher of science he managed to burst through the limits of science to a position of vantage outside or above it. Exploration of literature as a cosmos remains to be accomplished, though several high-powered rockets of literary theory have been sent forth in the last thirty years. We need to continue such exploration to discover the structure of its universe, its systematic categories. What I would like to see developed is a "cosmology" of literature, since I have now proposed that there are several universes in which we live and not merely a single "real" one. My assumption, I remind you, is that we can know nothing beyond our symbolic systems — that apart from them there is no reality, that what distinguishes us from the beasts, who live in a meaningless flux, is our ability to construct these systems. Reality, then, is that which has meaning, and there is no reality without meaning.

[1] Ernst Cassirer, *An Essay on Man*, New Haven, 1944, pp. 143–144.

II

Since we are talking about *verbal* universes, we might well begin by examining the nature of language in the literary cosmos. The most concise, clearest analysis of the nature of literary language, as against the discursive language of scientific method, occurs in Philip Wheelwright's *The Burning Fountain*.[2] Wheelwright is isolating the categories of the verbal literary universe from those of the discursive scientific realm. First, discursive language assumes that "a linguistic symbol is always distinct, symbol and referend are not interchangeable. There is nothing of twoness about the figure 2, the symbol is arbitrary." S. I. Hayakawa's famous little textbook *Language in Thought and Action* points out the difficulties inherent in any other view. The emperor's picture is not the emperor and need not in case of fire be removed from the building at the expense of life and limb. But literary language stubbornly insists on another attitude. Many symbols have their meaning in literature by *resembling*. The simplest example is the onomatopoetic word or phrase, as Pope demonstrates in his line on the Alexandrine,

That, like a wounded snake, drags its slow length along.

In poetry words are the primary *things*. When St. John says, "In the beginning was the Word," the poet takes him literally. Words are things, have the texture of things. Or to put it another way, it is only through the texture of words that things have texture at all.

Second, discursive language assumes that a symbol has on any occasion only one meaning. Ambiguity or overtones are consciously expunged as standing in the way of clarity. Literary language, on the other hand, thrives on ambiguity, overtones, and odd combinations of meaning. I am not referring here simply to tricks of syntax and puns but to a much broader conception of multi-meaning. In his provocative and often wildly fanciful book, *Seven Types of Ambiguity*, William Empson analyzes the various ways in which

2 Philip Wheelwright, *The Burning Fountain*, Bloomington, 1959, pp. 52ff.

literature operates ambiguously. They are, roughly, where "a word or a grammatical structure is effective in several ways at once," where "two or more meanings are resolved into one," where "two ideas are connected only by being both relevant in the context," where "two or more meanings of a statement do not agree among themselves, but combine to make clear a complicated state of mind," and so on. Empson's most famous example, his analysis of the first quatrain of Shakespeare's sonnet, is quoted in Chapter 4 in connection with my discussion of metaphysical poetry. Empson has been attacked for the outlandishness of many of his readings, for an *idée fixe*, but he has managed to point out one aspect of poetic language. Most contemporary critics, such as I. A. Richards and Cleanth Brooks, hold that some similar quality is typical of poetry. Richards emphasizes the quality of irony and Brooks the principle of paradox. In *The Well Wrought Urn* Brooks comments: "It is the scientist whose truth requires a language purged of every trace of paradox; apparently the truth which the poet utters can be approached only in terms of paradox." [3] Nor does Brooks claim he invented the theory of paradox. It is implicit in the comment of Coleridge on the activity of the imagination: ". . . [it] reveals itself in the balance or reconcilement of opposite or discordant qualities: of sameness, with difference; of the general, with the concrete; the idea, with the image; the individual, with the representative; the sense of novelty and freshness, with old and familiar objects." [4]

Third, discursive language assumes that a symbol can on any given occasion be clearly defined. Vagueness is error and "a lapse from the logical ideal." But literary language has a different standard of clarity, assuming that there are areas of experience where discursive exactness is actually vague and inaccurate. Literary language can sometimes express its object more precisely, as Wheelwright observes, by "a sort of controlled vagueness." This is true in much of the eighteenth-century poetry. An example is Gray's famous elegy, and it has been remarked of Blake that he is the liv-

---

3 *The Well Wrought Urn*, p. 3.
4 *Selected Poetry and Prose*, p. 275.

ing proof that poetic accuracy can be achieved with the use of vague words.

Fourth, discursive language demands that throughout a given discourse a word not change its meaning. But in literary language the symbol may accrete meanings as it repeats itself in any given work or body of work (as it does with Yeats' swans). Wheelwright provides us with several other contrasts between the two ways with language, but for our purposes here, I think, the principle of opposition is adequately illustrated.

III

If now we return to Kant we remember that he assumed the existence of what he called *a priori* forms of experience — space and time. The forms of space and time are subjective in that they are the eyeglasses which we can never remove, and they are objective in that we all wear them. We know that science in its various systems has developed a variety of spaces and times, that our raw everyday experience requires us to construct space and time in certain ways. These ways have one thing in common: when we talk about space and time we spatialize time, reduce it to workable measurability. We speak of spaces and lengths of time, we tell time by mechanical space metaphors like sundials and clocks. The French philosopher Henri Bergson objected to this tendency to spatialize time, since according to him the sheer experience of time is not measurable but qualitative. And yet his own metaphors for time are inevitably spatial — the wave in the ocean, the meteor, etc. Bergson was right in objecting to judgment of time only by measurement, but he was wrong, I think, in asking that we turn to our "real" experience of time. I doubt that there is any meaningful raw or "real" experience of time. What Bergson might better have advised was that we should fully experience the other forms of temporal and spatial construction (one of which is literature) in order to live the full life of time in all of its symbolic forms. As a philosopher Bergson was far outside the prevailing positivistic, scientific current. Other philosophers thought his prose too poetic, his language too vague, too ambiguous. He was making an effort to escape the constructions of the discursive universe and incorporate into his philosophy other symbolic universes and the values which they give to time. His error was to assume that there is meaningful raw experience rather than multiple universes. Bergson was wrong, but nearer right than the typical eighteenth-century philosopher, who saw the order of the universe only in terms of Newtonian science and analogues of it — Hartley's associationist psychology, for example. The tendency in that enlightened age was to impoverish experience by reducing all reality to the principles of this single system. And that is the danger of all single approaches to reality.

It is not to my purpose, nor am I competent, to discuss time conceptions in science or theology. What I am concerned with, as the *a priori* forms of the literary cosmos, are literary space and time. Let us begin with the problem of the time that elapses while one reads or while one observes a play. We know that in this respect literary time and clock time are totally different things. There was an attempt among some neoclassic critics (Castelvetro, for one) to insist on "unity of time" in the drama. A play's duration, they thought, should equal the time it takes for the events actually to occur in real life. This was manifestly absurd because so much successful drama had already been written in direct violation of it. We see at once that time as it passes in a play is different from time as it passes on the clock. The same may be true of space. The same stage can be several places at once, and spatial distance can be violated almost at will.

But this is only to begin our consideration. In the literary cosmos it is extremely difficult to locate action in time and space as we construct them according to the understanding. In Edmund Spenser's *Faerie Queene*, for example, the terrain is apparently both England and everywhere, and it is an England that never existed. The poet obviously makes his England both larger and smaller than the British Isles — larger because he universalizes his theme, smaller because he makes the whole of his universe emanate from the action which occupies his hero. His space is never map space and cannot be charted. His time is completely different from historic or clock time. We do not know *when* his action occurred. His archaic language distances the events from us, paradoxically so that they may return to us as both contemporary and timeless. Because they are not of *his* time they can just as well be of our time. The process is one of universalization. His time, also, within the work, does not pass according to the clock, but moves from qualitative peak to qualitative peak. Time is judged according to the import of the moment rather than according to the *amount* of it that has passed. This is not to say that Spenser's poem does not contain references to historical occurrences. The literary universe, though self-contained, can reach out and comment upon the other universes with which it lives. In Spenser this is done by an allegory which systematically refers to historical events. But this allegory is always enveloped by the larger form of the work and is but one of the particulars by which the total action is universalized.

Similarly an allegory like *Pilgrim's Progress* presents qualitative space, parts of space in that work having spiritual meanings. The work can be referred outward to theology, just as Spenser's poem can be referred outward to history; but in neither case is the world of the two works the world of the systems to which they partially direct our attentions. Their space and time have all the quality of the literary cosmos, and the reality in the poems is the reality of that cosmos, not that of history or theology. If we think otherwise we have to judge literary works by historical or theological standards, and both works will fade into insignificance in the face of better histories and theological works. Of course, literary worlds can have their own maps, though they need not. The fact that there is no map for the world of Kafka's *Castle* is one of its main formal characteristics. But the world of Sherlock Holmes is mapped out in words. And there can be hypothetical worlds with maps appended and genealogies provided, as in Tolkien's *The Lord of the Rings*, in which there is no relation to known history and geography. Even the creatures who inhabit that world are different from what we *know* to exist: hobbits, elves, gnomes, and ents. Though unreal by any external standard, Tolkien's world is real in its own formal categories, more real than the meaningless flux of daily activity previous to its organization into form, and meaningful to our lives.

The world of Tolkien is somewhat like the world of the typical literary utopia. A good many utopias, whether really "utopian" or ironic like Orwell's, place their worlds in the future of clock time. A little reflection, however, shows that infidelity to the outer world of experience in no way affects our acceptance of these utopian novels. When it becomes 1984 Orwell's book will not have lost its meaning if 1984, as history sees it, turns out to be unlike his depiction of it. Paradoxically, only if 1984 turns out to be as Orwell does describe it will his novel have become meaningless as a work of art. A novel which recaptures the past, as in Proust's *Remembrance of Things Past*, captures only the past of a consciousness which exists in the novel, not the past of history. Even in historical novels, which refer sometimes with considerable fidelity to the historic world of the past, there must be some principle which implies that the literary space and time of the novel are not history but literature, and the time of the novel is *essentially* no different from that of Spenser's *Faerie Queene*. A final illustration of the principle I am enunciating — and probably the best one — is the Bible, with its manifold levels of meaning, in which words like "Israel" and "Egypt," for example, present a variety of spatial and temporal suggestiveness which makes them contain their historical meanings rather than be imprisoned in them. A poet who tries to write a national epic for his own people will make great events happen in his own land. William Blake did not think that historically the British people were the lost tribes of Israel, even though a group called the British Israelites have interpreted his introductory song to *Milton* as an assertion that he did. Instead he was writing an epic. W. B. Yeats remarked:

> Blake does not think England the place of primitive humanity, or of the original wisdom. . . . He spoke of England and its past because he lived there. In the same way the folklore of the Echte hills in Galway says that the last judgment will be among those hills. Blake seeks the near and the particular always.[5]

[5] Quoted by Hazard Adams, *Blake and Yeats: The Contrary Vision*, Ithaca, 1955, p. 123.

When we consider these space-time projections in literature, we realize that they inevitably reflect Wheelwright's principles of literary language and vice versa. For example, the principle of multiple meaning offers us the possibility of a single symbolic structure, a literary universe so to speak, contained ideally by a single literary work.

IV

What would be the main characteristics of a literary cosmos operating according to the spatial and temporal forms and linguistic categories already mentioned? The center of such a cosmos is neither the sun nor the earth. Literary people are Copernican or Ptolemaic pretty much at will, without attention to science. The literary center is human and its cosmos expands in two directions at once (objective and subjective) from that center. The two directions mirror each other. The subjective world must be presented in the objects of the outer world, and that objective world has no meaning unless it is constantly referred back to the subjective. This is the reason that the categories of literary language are so similar to the categories of dream thought, as described by modern psychoanalysis. Freud pointed out that in the creation of the manifest dream:

> All the verbal apparatus by means of which the more subtle thought-relations are expressed, the conjunctions and prepositions, the variations of declension and conjugation are lacking, because the means of portraying them are absent: just as in primitive grammarless speech only the raw material of thought can be expressed, and the abstract is merged again in the concrete from which it sprang. . . . As a result of condensation one element in a manifest dream may correspond to a number of elements of the dream-thoughts.[6]

In his *Freudianism and the Literary Mind*, Hoffman puts the same idea this way: ". . . the latent dream does not enjoy the advan-

[6] Sigmund Freud, "Revision of the Theory of Dreams," *New Introductory Lectures*, London, 1933, p. 32.

tages of neat logical distinctions." He goes on to summarize how certain concepts appear in dreams:

And: the dream indicates the and-relationship in the form of simultaneity.

because, or *since:* the causal relationship is indicated by the juxtaposition of the "premise" dream with the "result" dream.

either-or: . . . either-or . . . becomes "both-and."

no, none, not: no does not appear to exist in the dream; is usually reduced to unity.

if: the conditional relation is represented by simultaneity; that is, not "if he should do this," but "when he did this." [7]

Modern psychology has, of course, been interested in the relation between dreams and mythology, and the relation of myth to literature has been explored by literary theorists. The investigations of Cassirer have brought to light some astonishingly interesting analogies between mythical thought and the literary cosmos. He writes:

To begin with the category of quantity . . . mythical thinking makes no sharp dividing line between the whole and its parts. . . . The part not only stands for the whole but positively is the whole.

In myth, then, space as we tend to *understand* it breaks down. But more important is the conception in myth of a whole system of analogies based upon the human body. The body is not, to the primitive, made from parts of the world; the world is made from parts of the human body, indeed the world is a human body. And the human being is, therefore, in the primitive view both the center and circumference of his universe. He lives in his universe and yet contains the ideas of it which are his systems. The literary cosmos has the same characteristics.

The extremes of man's imaginative powers mark the nadir and zenith of his literary universe. These extremes are often referred to as Heaven and Hell, but we can call them more generally, as Northrop Frye does, the limits of desire and repugnance.[8] These extremes

[7] Frederick J. Hoffman, *Freudianism and the Literary Mind*, New York, 1959, p. 40.
[8] Terms employed in *Anatomy of Criticism*.

are seldom fully explored in literature except in the most ambitious kind of literary work — the *Bible,* of course, Dante's *Divine Comedy,* Milton's *Paradise Lost* and *Paradise Regained,* and in another way Joyce's *Finnegans Wake.* Most literary reality exists between these two poles. And between them lies literary space and time. In this halfway world, space and time are seen as circular and cyclical, respectively. The archetype of human action in space is the quest, the archetype in time the passage through either the life of the individual or the community. In this world there are two areas and times. William Blake named them innocence and experience. The Bible called innocence Eden, and we usually call experience the world of nature. Human life is seen archetypally as a descent from one to the other and a journey or quest for the new paradise made desirable by the knowledge gained in experience.

The dominant themes of literature, whether romantic, tragic, satiric and ironic, or comic, are associated roughly with, respectively, the world of innocence, the fall from innocence to experience, the world of experience, and the ascent from experience to a higher imaginative world.

Desire (Heaven)

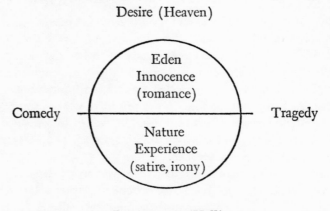

Repugnance (Hell)

In this concept of the literary cosmos we see that paradox is not merely a simple verbal device but a basic pattern. The quest in space and the human life in time are not reversible, and the only way to achieve the limit of desire is to descend very near to the limit of repugnance around the cycle. A central literary paradox is apparently therefore the paradox called that of the fortunate fall.[9] It is the central concept of Dante's *Divine Comedy*, of Milton's epics, and even of Baudelaire's lyric poetry.

The fact that the literary capture of desire involves a descent near to the limit of repugnance is one of the reasons that, as Coleridge observed, the disagreeable can be an aspect of the beautiful, that the simply agreeable is not necessarily the beautiful, that the beautiful must be described as a tension of opposing forces. Similarly, the Lord's display of Leviathan and Behemoth to Job in the Bible suggests the necessity of accepting the contraries in experience, the existence of the nadir as well as the zenith of the literary cosmos. The Lord's display to Job also suggests that His cosmos is constructed on the analogy of a literary work, but of course it would be more proper to say that the literary work is created on the analogy of God's creation. Coleridge's definition of the imagination makes the same point. He wrote: "The primary imagination I hold to be the living Power and prime Agent of all human Perception, and as a repetition in the finite mind of the eternal act of creation in the infinite I AM." [10] In those words and in his definition of the secondary imagination Coleridge proclaimed the artist to be the creator of a verbal universe, a world of words with its own laws. Coleridge held that to exercise the imagination was a moral imperative. That is the same moral imperative that the literary cosmos by its very existence demands: that one accept it as one of our realities. The alternative, it tells us, is to sink to its own nadir — the passive condition of thought which Coleridge called the fancy. In such a condition man is not a creator but has become, like Dante's Satan, encased in a block of ice with head hanging into the lonely abyss of the endless starry night of materialist science. For living only in *that* world he suffers Satan's torture. The world contains him — cold, forbidding, and without quality.

[9] See A. O. Lovejoy, "Milton and the Paradox of the Fortunate Fall," *Essays in the History of Ideas*, Baltimore, 1948.
[10] *Selected Poetry and Prose*, p. 268.

Some Suggested Reading

Bevan, Edwyn, *Symbolism and Belief*.
Cassirer, Ernst, *Essay on Man*.
Frye, Northrop, *Anatomy of Criticism*.
Wheelwright, Philip, *The Burning Fountain*.

Index

195

200